University
of Michigan
Business
School Management Series

INNOVATIVE SOLUTIONS TO THE
PRESSING PROBLEMS OF BUSINESS

The mission of the University of Michigan Business School Management Series is to provide accessible, practical, and cutting-edge solutions to the most critical challenges facing businesspeople today. The UMBS Management Series provides concepts and tools for people who seek to make a significant difference in their organizations. Drawing on the research and experience of faculty at the University of Michigan Business School, the books are written to stretch thinking while providing practical, focused, and innovative solutions to the pressing problems of business.

The Ethical Challenge

How to Lead with Unyielding Integrity

Noel M. Tichy
Andrew R. McGill

Editors

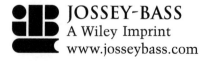

JOSSEY-BASS
A Wiley Imprint
www.josseybass.com

Published by Jossey-Bass
A Wiley Imprint
989 Market Street, San Francisco, CA 94103-1741   www.josseybass.com

Jossey-Bass books and products are available through most bookstores. To contact Jossey-Bass directly call our Customer Care Department within the U.S. at 800-956-7739, outside the U.S. at 317-572-3986 or fax 317-572-4002.

Jossey-Bass also publishes its books in a variety of electronic formats. Some content that appears in print may not be available in electronic books.

Library of Congress Cataloging-in-Publication Data

The ethical challenge : how to lead with unyielding integrity / Noel M. Tichy, Andrew R. McGill, editors.
    p. cm.— (University of Michigan Business School management series)
Includes index.
  ISBN 0-7879-6767-X (alk. paper)
  1. Business ethics—United States.   2. Leadership—Moral and ethical aspects—United States.   3. Integrity.   I. Tichy, Noel M. II. McGill, Andrew R., date.   III. Series.
  HF5387.E7745 2003
  174'.4—dc21
                       2003001612

Printed in the United States of America
FIRST EDITION
HB Printing   10 9 8 7 6 5 4 3 2 1

Contents

A Special Thanks

We are grateful to C. William Pollard, Jon Ward, and their ServiceMaster colleagues for sponsoring the 2002 Hansen-Wessner Memorial Lecture at the University of Michigan Business School.

That important event brought former Secretary of State James A. Baker III to Michigan only weeks after the full impact of the Enron scandal began to emerge. Baker's likening the transgressions of Enron to Watergate provided a wonderful perspective from which to build—ultimately leading to this book.

It is so fitting that Bill Pollard and ServiceMaster would be part of the genesis of a book on business ethics—something that both have been pillars at for decades. Their example of profiting not only from performance excellence but also the values they hold and live by provide a model for us all. We thank them.

Introduction

Teaching Your Values and Ethics Will Plant Them Across Your Organization

Noel M. Tichy, Andrew R. McGill

*Professors of Organizational Behavior
and Human Resource Management
University of Michigan Business School*

A cascade of public distrust—and disgust—has followed ethical transgressions by some of America's most visible business leaders, creating trauma on many fronts, none more critical than the need for leaders who can raise the level of business ethics—and spread the word.

Around the world, the need for leaders has never been greater. We are traversing terrain where weak or sleazy self-aggrandizers cannot carry us safely. We need smart, gutsy leaders with vision and integrity to get us through the minefields—leaders who can teach others to follow in their footsteps, hold firm to their values, and proliferate those norms across the organization. And, unfortunately, these leaders are in woefully short supply.

The Enron debacle, the demise of Arthur Andersen, questionable practices at Tyco, Sotheby's, Global Crossing, Qwest, WorldCom, Xerox, and a seemingly endless list of others, have pushed public regard for business and business leaders to new lows. The pervasive problems signal systemic rather than individual failures. The resulting lack of trust, the perception of greedy, self-dealing CEOs—sometimes appearing to be in collusion with Wall Street and public accounting firms—have driven investors out of the stock market in record numbers.

In some circles, the mere mention of Ken Lay of Enron, Bernie Ebbers of WorldCom, or a host of others—CEOs once heralded for their seeming genius—now elicits fervent cries for jail time and financial castigation.

The backdrop of a world geopolitically transformed, both symbolically and literally, by 9/11, with an aftermath of threats, ensuing battles in Afghanistan, plus escalating tensions around the world—the surge in terrorist bombings and military responses in the Middle East, saber-rattling confrontation by newest nuclear powers India and Pakistan, the government battling terrorist warlords in vast areas of the Philippines, rising nuclear tensions with North Korea, to name a frightening foursome—offers little relief and even less optimism. Around the world the need for leaders has never been greater.

This must change. And it will not be easy.

Getting business's ethical house in order starts with people. Consider that ethical transgressions can occur on countless levels. As social psychologists, we look at two variables: the environment and the person. Consider how your ethical miscues can affect people—employees, colleagues and superiors, suppliers, customers, internal regulators (lawyers, auditors, the board of directors), external regulators (government, interest groups, and the like), shareholders, or the public at large in your community. You can affect any or all, separately or combined, consciously or not. And you can have an impact on how they think of you in numerous ways—through corporate citizenship, product quality, your business plans and strategy, how openly and candidly you communicate, by the clarity of your business reviews and reports—internally and externally, by the transparency of your financial and other public statements, and you certainly have an impact on your image if you commit premeditated fraud or deceit, or even violate criminal laws. These can be acts of commission—or acts of omission, venial—in the moral theologian's view—or mortal.

And that only scratches the surface. Yet with so many opportunities and audiences with which to cross the ethical line, attempting to define or legislate proper behavior is impossible. Some legal absolutes can be defined. But real ethical behavior and understanding can only result when the right norms and examples are shared and internalized by an organization's leaders.

■ What Is a Real "Win"?

It can start with us, our colleagues at the University of Michigan Business School and the wider Michigan community, business leaders committed to making things better, and—in a small way—this book. In taking that step toward building better business leaders, we can start by changing some of our own ideas about what it means to "win"—the executive heroes we anoint, the cases we classicize, the profit leaders we cheer, the new-idea wizards we celebrate—all without knowing whether their wins were clean or dirty, contrived or real.

That's the Enron lesson. For just as the right business ethics must focus on the long term, so must the right examples represent the best in true ideas, values, and performance—not in any single day, week, month, quarter, or even year, but over the long haul. These are the winners—models for the future—we should share and aim to shape in our students. This book was born in that long-term commitment, to help develop a new generation of world-class business leaders with unyielding integrity—leaders who will be able to keep generating more such leaders as their careers progress.

These leaders are essential if we are to retain and enhance our free enterprise system. But even the best leaders won't be sufficient for that task without properly defined ethical limits, a rule of law on intellectual property, and transparency and trust in financial disclosures. The current system's response to miscues of the early 2000s—albeit with too much hype and some overreaction—will help with this part of the equation.

But at best (as General Electric CEO Jeffrey Immelt told Charlie Rose) that sets "the low bar"—too low a standard. Leadership, Immelt said, must be about high performance and high values. And values don't come from some vacuum, they result from a strong heritage of trust and integrity—an internal transparency of the value of integrity, leaders who have clear Teachable Points of View on integrity, who can effectively teach them to leaders at all levels of their organizations.

It starts with leaders' getting their stories right. To help people in the organization internalize your core values—to compel their attention, grab them emotionally, challenge them to raise the ethical bar—all business leaders at the beginning of the twenty-first century need to have a *Teachable Point of View* (TPOV, for short) about their business in general and business ethics in particular—what they will and won't do, values and absolutes for their organization, examples they model—so their employees can follow suit.

This book is a challenge to executives, business students, and leaders in all institutions to clarify their own Teachable Point of View on ethics and integrity. We also ask that you, as the reader, engage with us in a workshop—do a series of "Exercises on Ethics" as you reflect on what the authors represented here (key leaders, academics, and students)—say about the topic. These exercises will form the building blocks of your personal Teachable Point of View on business ethics. They will require you to wrestle with the big issues yourself—something we'll help make happen as you read, reflect, and then do.

■ Developing Your TPOV on Business Ethics

It takes four basic building blocks to get started on your Teachable Point of View:

- *Ideas:* Great companies are built on ideas. By passing ideas to others and teaching others how to develop good ideas, leaders create organizations that are fine-tuned to deliver success. These ideas can provide the answer to questions such as Where are we going? What are we aiming to accomplish?
- *Values:* Winning leaders articulate values explicitly and shape them to support their business ideas, but always in the context of the times. Or, as GE Chairman Jeffrey Immelt says, "Now more than ever before, people want to win, but they want to do it with heart, and both things are important in a twenty-first-century company. You have got to find a way to attract people who know how to give back to the environment, and give back to the community, and give back to the workplace."

- *Emotional Energy:* Winning leaders have a clear set of beliefs and actions for motivating others to buy in to and internalize the values of the organization. Winning leaders are also motivated and they motivate others about change and transitions. Leaders energize others when they personally interact with them.
- *Edge:* Great leadership is about making tough yes/no decisions. Winning leaders face reality, and then make the hard decisions about people, products, businesses, customers, and suppliers.

All successful business leaders must be able to articulate their own Teachable Point of View on business ethics and drive it through their organization, to engage others to teach the same values lessons to their people, to build a values-based culture across the organization, to ensure that—unlike the situation at Enron and others—everyone knows the ethical line and is neither shy nor silent if people risk crossing it.

Every one of us has critical life events that have shaped who we are today. These can form important building blocks to your TPOV. Think about the important lessons and experiences that have shaped your own values as a leader:

- *Ethical and moral development:* What shaped your own values—things important in your family as you were growing up, lessons learned in school or your place of worship, experiences with friends in social activities or sports, formative learning from travel, work, education, community citizenship, and so forth?
- *Societal and cultural development:* What social and cultural events shaped your development, helping build the values you hold today? War? Racism? Sexism? Discrimination? Religious persecution? Economic separation? Also, experientially, being laid off, arrested, out of money, without transportation?

- *Corporate conformity:* What values and ideas have been shaped by the culture of your own organization or profession—no bad news, no big risks, no novel ideas, no challenging your superiors? Or customers are out to get you, yelling to summon subordinates, making the numbers no matter what?

- *Shaping your leadership:* What things most influenced the values and ethics you hold as a leader today? Why or how did they impact you? What have you done differently because of them? How could you share those lessons to help in the development of your own people?

- *Facing tough dilemmas:* What are the big ethical dilemmas you have faced, especially in business? How did you work through them? Did you deliberate privately, or share your challenge with others? What are your big take-away lessons? How have they influenced the way you lead today? How would you share those lessons to be instructive to others?

■ Building Virtuous Teaching Cycles on Ethics

As you think through those issues and the others they trigger, key elements that can form parts of your Teachable Point of View will come to life. When leaders personalize things—share a past experience or even make themselves a bit vulnerable—it adds to the credibility of their message. People need reminders that their leaders were once in the trenches, too.

This exercise gives most leaders a wealth of potential material from which to craft messages on business ethics. What messages are critical to send? How do you want people to behave? How should they think through ethical dilemmas? How much flexibility do they have to balance competing values?

This book will help you hone these elements into your Teachable Point of View on business ethics.

As these lessons are taught again and again, what can develop within an organization is a pattern of Virtuous Teaching Cycles, in which the sharing of ideas in all directions results in knowledge creation (see Figure I.1).

The core of the process, detailed in Tichy's new book *The Cycle of Leadership: How Great Leaders Teach Their Organizations to Win* (HarperCollins, 2002), emphasizes that

- Knowledge creation and organizational learning are greatest when leaders—up to and including the CEO—see themselves as teachers who share their points of view and see this process as an essential part of their leadership.
- The richness of such teaching interchanges—back and forth, in search of knowledge—breeds more teaching across the organization, producing a cycle of leadership.

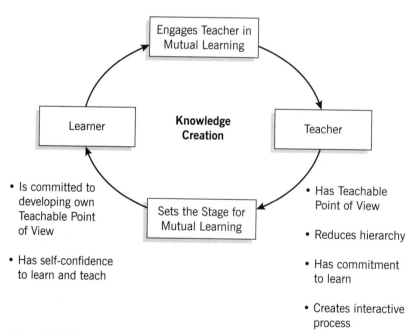

Figure I.1. **Virtuous Teaching Cycles.**

- That learning, teaching, and sharing maximizes an organization's knowledge creation and better prepares leaders for higher-impact leadership roles in the future.

The cycle of learning is powerful and engaging as it proliferates through an organization. The more it engages people, the more it replicates itself, with more and more people teaching the key ethical lessons, putting dilemmas on the table to be openly considered and debated, sharing experiences—both best and worst practices.

Leaders comfortable dealing with such challenges from a strong ethical platform will become the corporate leaders of tomorrow. Listen to the importance some of today's most influential business leaders place on attracting people with such business ethics:

- *Warren Buffett, CEO, Berkshire Hathaway:* "In looking for people to hire, you look for three qualities: integrity, intelligence and energy. And if they don't have the first, the other two will kill you. You think about it; it's true. If you hire somebody without the first, you really want them to be dumb and lazy. . . . Contemplating any business act, an employee should ask himself whether he would be willing to see it immediately described by an informed and critical reporter on the front page of his local paper, there to be read by his spouse, children, and friends . . . we simply want no part of any activities that pass legal tests, but that we, as citizens, would find offensive. . . . It takes 20 years to build a reputation, and five minutes to ruin it. If you think about that, you'll do things differently."

- *Hank McKinnell, CEO, Pfizer:* "Our company is thoroughly grounded in our values. They begin with a prized personal and organizational quality—integrity—and end with a shared concern for community. Our values include leadership, innovation, performance, teamwork, customer focus, and respect for people.

These values guide every decision we make, everywhere. . . . Enron's collapse at the end of 2001 pushed companies to examine all aspects of corporate governance. I want to clearly affirm Pfizer's commitment to integrity in all our dealings and everywhere we operate. Our colleagues at all levels are firmly grounded in Pfizer's values, with integrity first and foremost among them."

- *Jack Welch, Retired CEO, GE:* "It's the first and most important of our values. Integrity means always abiding by the law, both the letter and the spirit. But it's not just about laws; it is at the core of every relationship we have. Inside the company, integrity establishes the trust that is so critical to the human relationships that make our values work. With trust, employees can take risks and believe us when we say a 'miss' doesn't mean career damage. With trust, employees can stretch performance goals and can believe us when we promise that falling short is not a punishable offense. Integrity and trust are at the heart of the informality we cherish. There are no witnesses needed to conversations, nor the need to 'put it in writing.' None of that— our word is enough. . . . A period of transition is a period of change, and some of our values will be modified to adapt to what the future brings. One will not [change]: Our commitment to integrity, which beyond doing everything right, means always doing the right thing."

■ Developing the Next Generation of Leaders

Our leadership tank is low. We are not producing enough leaders at all levels, especially at senior and CEO levels. Consider the blue-chip companies in the past decade that have had to find outside candidates to replace their departing CEOs: Merck, EDS, AT&T (twice), HP, 3M, Home Depot. And there are scores more.

This is a terrible track record when perhaps the No. 1 responsibility of a CEO is to develop other leaders who can carry on the legacy of the organization.

Our leadership pipelines are broken—in politics, diplomacy, and religious and social organizations, as well as in business. Even when organizations do select insiders to take over the top spot, they often have to settle for players who lack the needed leadership skills. And these inadequate leaders are unable to drive the needed transformations or develop others to be leaders. Thus they suffer both performance problems in the short term and a continuing leadership crises in the long term, leaving our society and economy vulnerable.

To deal head-on with this challenge, incoming MBAs in the University of Michigan Business School Class of 2004 experienced the business ethics challenge firsthand—as the very first thing they did in the school year. Each student was assigned the task of analyzing and writing about the biggest ethical challenge in their own career. Their roster of ethical miscues was not unlike what you'd find with a group of seasoned business executives—pressure to pad the numbers, cheating on quality checks, using insider information to take special advantage, and the like.

That exercise was the kickoff to a week-long MBA Orientation that dealt squarely with business ethics issues from beginning to end, from morning till night.

Some of the country's most influential CEOs shared their thoughts with students in an open dialogue: Jeff Immelt of GE, Jim Hackett of Steelcase, Joe Liemandt of Trilogy, and co-founder Eleanor Josaitis of Focus: HOPE.

So important was the event that it brought out some of the school's most respected faculty: Dean Bob Dolan and professors Kim Cameron, Brent Chrite, Tim Fort, Bob Quinn, and Anjan Thakor joined us in launching the ethics program.

The results proved a natural to be coupled with a Service-Master-sponsored spring event for students and faculty at the business school, "Business Ethics in Skeptical Times," in which former Secretary of State James A. Baker III cautioned against overreacting to the miscues at Enron and beyond, but stressed the importance of values in making the right calls under such circumstances. ServiceMaster Chairman Emeritus William Pollard and Chairman and CEO Jonathan Ward emphasized the importance of values in their culture. And New York Leadership Academy CEO Robert Knowling Jr. and Michigan professor C.K. Prahalad underscored the importance of such a set of "core ethics" to guide their most challenging decisions.

These perspectives provided a backdrop not only for launching the incoming MBAs on their own quest to develop their Teachable Point of Views on business ethics but for building this book.

■ The Michigan TPOV on Business Ethics

The MBA forum for this ethics learning was the Leadership Development Program, a wide-ranging, thought-provoking experience that engages students around the critical issues affecting business—an ongoing process over their two years at UMBS. Students were challenged to develop their own Teachable Points of View on being a businessperson who operates ethically, with a personal commitment to help renew public faith in business.

The core principle is that leaders must be people of integrity who are able to work in teams, understand diversity, have a clearly developed set of values, and have the ability to articulate their leadership agenda in their personal TPOV. Students think through their

- *Values homework:* Key values and ethics they want to stress in their TPOV, with rationale and examples, based on analysis of their own ethical dilemmas in business.

- *Life experiences:* Related life experiences, in both their personal and business lives, to provide examples of real-world activities that have been ethically challenging.
- *Macro context:* Positioning of the student's own experiences and values dilemmas in the larger context of providing leadership and direction to their organization—and fitting the pieces together.
- *Role models:* Best role models, whose experiences in values and ethics dilemmas serve as vivid examples of how to wrestle with the issues—a model to be developed as part of their TPOV to provide an in-depth example.

With those issues sorted out, the students then discussed what it takes to be a leader in the community of the University of Michigan Business School. Here's what they concluded it takes to be a Michigan Leader:

- *Leadership integrity:* Personal, interpersonal, team, organizational, and societal; the unyielding type practiced by the best companies and leaders in the world.
- *Lead and develop globally diverse teams:* Learning to master teamwork among diverse people is a key element of the MBA experience, both among MBAs and through citizenship projects in the community.
- *Global mindset:* Framing business issues in the complex, changing global geopolitical landscape is a challenge that must become commonplace for true global leaders.
- *Leadership Teachable Point of View:* Integrating your MBA learnings into a personal comprehensive set of ideas, values, and ways of energizing others, as well as gaining the courage and edge to make tough calls.
- *Global corporate citizenship:* Developing a clear Teachable Point of View on environmental issues: land, air, water, and biodiversity; human capital issues such as housing, health care,

education, and jobs; and a point of view on what the role of business should be in this arena.

We cannot stress the global citizenship element too strongly. The moral imperative to give back to society is essential for a just society. And as Peter Drucker says, "Citizenship in and through the social sector is not a panacea for the ills of post-capitalist society, but it may be a prerequisite for tackling these ills. It restores the civic responsibility that is the mark of citizenship, and the civic pride that is the mark of community."

And the need for such action doesn't stop at the U.S. shores. While business scandals may have diminished the U.S. role as a global benchmark, they also presented future business leaders with a compelling challenge. Sustainable development around the globe depends on wealth-producing businesses' delivering financial performance with integrity. We need great leaders across all sectors of society to help.

This need is not new.

■ Citizenship Reinforces Ethics

In our long study of leadership and citizenship, we have come to believe that no institution—religious, military, educational, political, or business—can be great unless it has a great leader at the top, with great values and ethics, who teaches and develops leaders at all levels of the organization. The goal is to have leaders at all levels who all teach and develop other leaders.

We have been disappointed many times—by national leaders, health-care leaders, and business leaders. The scale seems tipped in favor of more failed leaders than great ones. But there is hope. Some wonderful role models can help us move the other way. Societal change agents such as Martin Luther King Jr. and

Mother Teresa in India were among the best—inspirations, although we never met them.

And we have had the privilege and honor to work with other world-class leaders, including the late Father William Cunningham and his Focus: HOPE co-founder Eleanor Josaitis, as well as GE's Jeff Immelt, and Trilogy's Joe Liemandt. Their words on leadership and ethics in business will leave you in no doubt where they stand.

■ About This Book

You'll meet them and more great teachers with great ethics in this book. It is structured in three sections:

- *Part One* frames the business ethics challenge in the context of the events of 2001 in the aftermath of the Enron debacle. A detailed history recounts the Enron story, enabling readers to experience step-by-step how the company passed the point of no return. A ServiceMaster-sponsored event brought former Secretary of State James A. Baker III, CEO Robert Knowling of the New York Leadership Academy, ServiceMaster's William Pollard and Jonathan Ward, and UMBS Professor C. K. Prahalad to the Michigan Business School in mid-2002, and their wise and enriching words, plus a plea for more than platitudes from Dean Bob Dolan, help frame the issue.
- *Part Two* recites, as they did with incoming MBAs in Fall 2002 Orientation at the University of Michigan Business School, the experiences and dilemmas on business ethics of some of America's most influential CEOs—Jeff Immelt of GE, Jim Hackett of Steelcase, and Joe Liemandt of Trilogy. Commentary on the same issues comes from some of the

most thoughtful UMBS faculty members—Anjan Thakor, Robert Quinn, Kim Cameron, and Tim Fort.

- *Part Three* takes the issue of business ethics to its logical conclusions, with Michigan MBA students wrestling with their own ethical dilemmas—as they did in their Class of 2004 Orientation—and our emphasizing and building on the importance of corporate global citizenship as a core ethics issue. Focus: HOPE co-founder Eleanor Josaitis and William Davidson Institute Managing Director Brent Chrite share in the challenges in expanding citizenship—locally and globally.

All the sources whose words you will consider are leaders with vision and courage, but more important, they are models for the future—leader-teachers who created Virtuous Teaching Cycles as a natural part of their leadership styles: namely, leading by teaching and teaching interactively, in a way that both they and their students learn. Even if you don't necessarily agree with them, their methods as teachers provide good starting road maps.

When it comes to business ethics, we need such great teachers.

One lesson we hope leaders will take from this book is that once they start to apply the concept of a Virtuous Teaching Cycle, they must wrestle with the issue of scale. Leaders of large organizations must create the conditions for thousands of people to engage in Virtuous Teaching Cycles. The other impact we hope this book has on readers is to start them looking at the world through the lens of Virtuous Teaching Cycles.

We also should recognize the fine teachers with great values who routinely learn and teach and are already part of our lives. Really, they are everywhere—parents who both teach and learn from their children. Good music and art teachers do the same. Likewise, in medicine, great clinical faculty learn from their residents. The U.S. military's Special Operations Forces personnel operate this way, always teaching and learning from each other, regardless of rank.

■ A Pair of Great Leaders

Here are two of the best examples we know of leaders who exemplify the leader-teacher role—people who serve as models of the highest ethics:

- *Wayne Downing, who transformed the Special Operations Forces (SOF) and made it a teaching organization.* As the four-star general leading this organization, he spent the majority of his time in the field teaching and learning from his troops at all levels. He transformed the SOF from a singularly focused cold-war entity to a multifaceted team of leaders with humanitarian aid skills in addition to awesome combat abilities. After 9/11, President Bush named Downing special assistant and the deputy national security adviser for combating terrorism. Noel Tichy has been to the Navy SEALs school, which was under Downing's command, and personally spent time with the leaders he helped develop. Their interactions with him are very rich. Even in retirement, Downing remains a leader-teacher.
- *Eleanor Josaitis, who co-founded Focus: HOPE in 1968 in Detroit with Father William Cunningham.* She has been unstoppable in her pursuit of its mission, which at its essence is "intelligent and practical solutions to racism, poverty and injustice." Her leadership, along with that of her co-founder, the late Father Cunningham, has built a six-hundred-person organization that is emulated around the world, but so far never to the same scale.

Focus: HOPE provides food for 42,600 people a month, trains machinists, runs a for-profit machine tool business, has a program allowing students to earn bachelor's degrees in engineering, runs a child-care center and a Montessori school, offers remedial education to high school graduates and dropouts, and has an information technology training center, as well. It does this on a modern forty-acre campus created in the bombed-out, burned-out area of inner-city Detroit.

Eleanor Josaitis teaches every day of her life. She starts each morning by walking the factory floor at 6 A.M. She also makes sure that she interviews every new colleague, with whom she shares her Teachable Point of View on poverty, racism, and the role of Focus: HOPE. She does this over and over again with all stakeholders. She *lives* the Virtuous Teaching Cycle.

Both Downing and Josaitis are obviously well aware of what former Honeywell CEO Larry Bossidy concluded after his decades in business, most in high leadership roles, on leaders sharing their views on business ethics with those who are following in their footsteps. Said Bossidy: "You won't remember when you retire what you did in the first quarter . . . or the third. What you'll remember is how many people you developed, how many people you helped have a better career because of your interest and your dedication to their development. . . . When confused as to how you're doing as a leader, find out how the people you lead are doing. You'll know the answer."

Exercises in Ethics

In the post–Enron world, many leaders—among them GE's Jeff Immelt—contend that merely obeying the law sets the "low bar" for business and that real leaders must do more.

1. What standards of ethics and integrity do you have for your organization that go beyond just obeying the law?

_____

_____

_____

_____

2. Think about some of the critical life events that shaped your own ethical development—and list a few important ones in each of the following categories:

a. *Ethical and moral development*—family values, school, religion, friends, sports, social activities, travel, work, education, community citizenship. . . .

_____

_____

_____

_____

_____

_____

_____

_____

_____

_____

_____

b. *Societal and cultural development*—war, racism, sexism, discrimination, religious persecution, economic separation, layoffs, arrests, poverty, lack of mobility. . . .

_____

_____

_____

_____

_____

_____

_____

_____

_____

_____

_____

c. *Corporate conformity*—norms in the culture of your own organization and profession. . . .

_____

_____

_____

_____

_____

_____

_____

_____

d. *Shaping your leadership*—things that most influenced the ethics you hold as a leader today. . . .

_____

_____

_____

_____

_____

_____

_____

_____

e. *Facing tough dilemmas*—big ethical problems that you have faced—especially in business—and how you dealt with them. . . .

_____

_____

_____

_____

_____

_____

_____

_____

PART 1

The Abuse

Bolstered by post-Watergate demands for stronger business ethics and integrity, U.S. corporations sought enhanced diversity on their boards of directors and in other
forms of internal oversight, while government toughened external regulations and oversight. These added protections
seemed sure to prevent a repeat of the transgressions of the past,
so business got back to what it does best—doing business.

In the 1990s, an unprecedented economic boom—best il-
lustrated by record stock prices and an enormous expansion of
"paper wealth" across American society—directed our attention
(if not envy) to the growing list of emerging dot-com billionaires.
We reveled in the renewed spirit of the American dream.

That came to a halt with the turn of the century. First came the dot-com crash. Then, as 2001 drew to a close, the aftermath of the collapse of Enron featured confessions by scores of American corporations to a variety of ethical abuses. It was clear that we as a society needed to pay greater attention to ethics and integrity in business—and to getting our ethical house in order.

Part One begins by going through the Enron story step by step, looking at what went wrong and how each step appeared to beget a worse one, as Professor Andrew R. McGill recounts the last year in the life of Enron. That chapter is followed by six based on a special seminar on ethics sponsored by one American corporation committed to strong ethics, ServiceMaster. The seminar was held at the University of Michigan Business School and introduced by past and present ServiceMaster chairmen C. William Pollard and Jonathan Ward. Former Secretary of State James A. Baker III, while condemning the transgressions of Enron, finds strengths in the self-correcting nature of capitalism, something he likens to the self-repairing nature of democracy that he experienced as the top U.S. diplomat. Finally, Professor C. K. Prahalad and business executive Robert Knowling share their perspectives on ethics in business. University of Michigan Business School Dean Robert Dolan admonishes us to move forward not with more rhetoric, but with more good deeds.

Business Ethics Reality Stunned Americans as Enron, Others Misled Investors and Employees

Andrew R. McGill

Associate Professor of Organizational Behavior and Human Resource Management University of Michigan Business School n the winter of 2001, just a few months after the 9/11 attacks on New York and Washington, another frightening spectacle began to unfold in America. During the six months that started that November, scores of Fortune 500 companies stepped forward to confess a huge array of legal and ethical misdeeds, from filing misleading financial reports to out-and-out premeditated fraud.

While the restatements of profits at many companies—and the actual demise of a few—didn't kill thousands of people or send American soldiers into combat, they directly touched the lives of hundreds of thousands of people. Stock prices plummeted. Small retirement nest eggs and large fortunes were lost. Thousands of workers were laid off. CEOs were fired as company after company admitted to unethical and sometimes illegal activities.

More important, most of the culprits were not little entrepreneurial start-ups. The Internet bubble had burst eighteen months earlier. The little guys who may have been playing fast and loose were already gone. Now it was huge corporations and old-line auditing firms who were admitting to ethical lapses. The breadth and depth of the problems made it seem as though the moral fiber of mainstream American business was unraveling. The result was a loss of public confidence not only in corporations and executives but in the checks and watchdogs that were supposed to ensure their honesty.

This loss of confidence is the critical issue facing leaders in both the private and the public sectors today, as business struggles to recover from its lowest ranking in public esteem since surveys have been taken. America's ability to maintain a healthy democratic society and a free-market economy requires leaders who can reestablish public trust by building institutions that are firmly and clearly grounded in the highest ethical standards.

The particulars of each company's story are different. The moral failings vary in scope and severity. Merck boosted its revenues by including prescription fees actually paid to dispensing pharmacies. Several of Wall Street's finest were caught touting a stock in one part of their organization while their investment arm was dumping the same stock. WorldCom placed extreme values on businesses it acquired—to the tune of scores of billions—to boost its stock price, then executives sold. But no company's problems, in depth and complexity, surpassed those of the company that started the spiraling ethical dive—Enron. Exploring Enron's black hole is instructive as an in-depth example of how borderline-reasonable policies can so easily cross the line. Oversight lost becomes an invitation to cheat—a practice that, once begun, can become pervasive. The Enron story serves not only as the historical last straw leading to much tougher standards—inside and out—for business transparency but also as a symbolic warning for future managers of how not to get sucked in.

Enron was an old-line Texas energy company turned fast-track growth darling. It was the country's seventh-largest business in revenues at the turn of the century and in 2001—in the wake of the Internet bust of 2000—it was one of Wall Street's few remaining stars. In reality, beneath the veneer, Enron was a company with terminal financial woes—woes masked by misdeeds, manipulation, and downright lies.

Enron, with its unabashed self-image as the "world's greatest company," was created in the mid-1980s merger of two pipeline companies, Houston Natural Gas and InterNorth. The new company expanded into untraditional and lucrative businesses from long-term energy contracts to brokering energy trades to speculation in energy futures, and even to derivative-like energy products, with dreams of more built around the Internet. But, as in most entrepreneurial businesses, many of Enron's wild-eyed start-ups lost money. And those mounting losses built growing obstacles to Enron's fulfilling something even more important than its flashy reputation: its increasingly ambitious quarterly growth and profit targets, which fueled its stock price and made the empire possible.

In a sleight-of-hand maneuver to cover those mounting start-up losses, Enron crossed the line. While some debate the legality of what Enron did next, even the most charitable would struggle to find anything redeeming in a plan designed to deliberately mislead investors.

■ Project Summer: The Imperative Quest for New Money

In retrospect, the first signs of Enron's financial woes came in the summer of 2000, ironically as its stock price—unlike the scores plummeting in the Internet bust—was heading toward its all-time high of $90.56 a share. Enron was in dire need of cash and looked for a solution in "Project Summer," a plan to unload about $6 billion to $8 billion in scattered international projects, so the company could concentrate on energy trading and building a new broadband communications business. With its debt mounting and a cash crisis on the horizon, Enron saw an opportunity to save the day by packaging a collection of its troubled and often poorly performing international assets to sell to a consortium of wealthy Middle East investors, led by a special adviser to the longtime president of the United Arab Emirates.

"It was a monstrously complex deal," one former Enron official told the *New York Times*, citing different sets of ownership rules, banking covenants, and legal restrictions for each foreign property—with heated debates inside and outside about which Enron holdings would ultimately make up the package. "This would have been the largest transaction of its type ever done in the global energy business."

But it was not to be. Because most of the more than $7 billion had been raised from the royal families of the United Arab Emirates, the president, Sheik Zayed bin Sultan al-Nahayan, needed to approve the deal. But, at the last minute, negotiations broke down when Sheik Zayed was hospitalized with kidney problems—ultimately flying to the United States for a kidney transplant and treatment for a fractured hip—and the deal could not be revived in time for Enron to avert a cash crunch, former executives told the *Times*.

Instead, the company pushed a group of top executives to sell smaller pieces of Enron's international holdings, to strengthen its balance sheet and bolster its credit rating. When there were no takers, former Enron executives said, Chief Financial Officer Andrew Fastow began exploiting an investment partnership angle he had developed several years before—initially under tight board approval and oversight—to "sell" the foreign assets to a variety of off-balance-sheet partnerships, temporarily buffing up the year-end financial picture.

These new Fastow partnerships would be far different from the early ones, when outside board members—former National Security Adviser Brent Scowcroft; Thomas Theobald, the former vice chairman of Citibank and CEO of Continental Bank of Chicago; and George Slocum, former CEO of Transco Energy—personally oversaw the deals between Enron and any affiliates. Those deals were an early example of Enron's aggressive financial techniques and, like later ones, were designed to keep high-debt assets such as power plants off Enron's balance sheet—but the earlier deals were carefully scrutinized by Enron's outside lawyers, auditors, and directors. So when Fastow had been permitted by the board to run his first such partnership in the early 1990s, investors were warned that the dealings would be less than arm's length. Or, as an early prospectus acknowledged, "Enron will control the company and will have extensive ongoing relationships with the company. Certain conflicts of interest exist and may arise in the future as a result of these relationships."

Even so, an Enron Global Power and Pipelines executive warned Enron's chief executive of perceived conflicts and irregularities, with "deal makers enriching themselves to the company's detriment," according to the *New York Times*. Others said the complaining executive was overzealous, that any conflicts were disclosed, and nothing further was said inside Enron on the subject—director Theobald recalling, "We took our job seriously" and "demanded total arm's-length dealing."

Global Power was later spun off by Enron, only to be reacquired three years later. And the complaining Enron executive quit in 2000 "after a two-day migraine headache" to attend Yale Divinity School.

■ The Anatomy of Enron's Partnerships

The new Fastow partnerships were far different.

"Fastow's tricky partnerships were bailing out the company," a former executive told the *Times*. "These big transactions take six to nine months to do, minimum. Fastow could close one in two to three weeks. His people didn't have to do due diligence."

It was another year before Fastow took the fall for creating the less-monitored, off-balance-sheet partnerships—partnerships from which he personally profited privately to upwards of $30 million. Enron's very misleading financial reporting was old hat by then.

By September 2001, Enron was disguising money that had all the earmarks of a new loan from J.P. Morgan Chase, carrying it instead as cash assets and liabilities from Enron's trading business. This so-called *structured finance* involved the bank's delivering $350 million to a Channel Islands company in exchange for a future payment based on the variable value of gas futures six months later. The Channel Islands firm then agreed to a deal with Enron on exactly the same terms—passing on to Enron the $350 million in cash—resulting in a "circular transaction" in which many of the obligations simply cancelled each other out. With one exception: Enron agreed to repay Morgan six months later the fixed amount of $356 million—the equivalent of 3.4 percent interest, the going rate at the time.

Records held by longtime Enron auditor Arthur Andersen show that Enron received $3.9 billion between 1992 and 2001, at least $2.5 billion of it in the three years before declaring bankruptcy, in similar large loans from Wall Street firms. Fastow "was almost somewhat threatening" in demanding that the big banks invest in his partnerships, according to one insider, threatening that Enron would not use their banking or investment banking services if they didn't participate. The loans, which helped mask Enron's weakening financial condition, were in addition to the $8 billion to $10 billion in long- and short-term debt Enron did disclose on its financial statements. Revealing its true debt would have given credit rating agencies, analysts, and investors much earlier signs that Enron was far riskier than appeared—making it much harder and more expensive to raise the billions required to fuel Enron's fast growth.

"Considering that our credit rating was largely based on information now deemed by the company itself to be misleading, inaccurate, and false, it is pretty likely that the credit rating would have been different" for Enron, a Moody's Investors Service official told the *Times*. Perhaps. But Moody's, Standard & Poor's, and Fitch were all aware that the partnership trusts related to Enron had made financial commitments tied to Enron's stock price—and that if the stock fell below certain trigger thresholds, it could require the company to pay more than $3.3 billion. Despite activating those triggers in May and again in September 2001, it was not until mid-October that any of the big three credit rating agencies began to warn of Enron's deteriorating financial condition—and not until late November, just days before its bankruptcy, that they actually lowered Enron's debt rating below "investment grade."

Newer rules in the aftermath of Enron now require such hedges to also be accounted for as loans. In fact, Credit Suisse

First Boston—like J.P. Morgan Chase and Citigroup, a big lender to the Enron partnerships—"booked the transactions as a loan," a spokesman told the *Times*, adding, "it was like a floating-rate loan." Enron, in contrast, called the loans "assets from price risk management" and, to a far lesser extent, accounts receivable, an Andersen spokesman told the *Times*. Repayments that Enron owed the banks were listed as "liabilities from price risk management" with a small amount as accounts payable. A Senate committee later concluded that Citigroup and J.P. Morgan Chase deliberately helped Enron effectively borrow money while not disclosing it to investors. "Enron loves these deals as they are able to hide funded debt from their equity analysts," a Chase banker wrote in an e-mail message quoted by the *Times*.

The Citigroup transactions went a step further, as Citi hedged itself against losses on $2.4 billion of its Enron loans—by effectively buying insurance through other derivative trades, much as a small-time bookie might lay off a large bet. "Citigroup set up trusts to sell securities called 'linked Enron obligations' and 'credit-linked notes,' for which investors paid $2.4 billion in principal," the *Times* reported. "Both types of securities paid a constant return unless Enron missed a payment to Citigroup or went bankrupt. In that case, Citigroup would take the investors' principal and replace it with a slice of Enron's debt with the same face value. An investor who held $100,000 worth of the notes when Enron filed for bankruptcy would have received $100,000 in debt issued by Enron," worth pennies on the dollar at best.

"Close readers of Enron's financial statements would have seen the lines identified as assets and liabilities from price risk management in the assets and liabilities sections," the *Times* wrote. "These lines grew far faster than the quantities of commodities traded by the company. From the fourth quarter of 1999 to the first quarter of 2001, price risk management grew to $22 billion from roughly $5 billion in assets and liabilities."

While apparently within accounting regulations at the time, such transactions underscore the aggressive nature of Enron's quest for cash, all the while attempting to represent the transactions as new business investments rather than mounting debts—through partnerships that Enron's own board investigators later concluded, according to the *Times,* "served no economic purpose other than to manipulate reported profits. An independent third party would never have entered into such dealings." A bankruptcy examiner's later report found that between 1997 and 2001, Enron had received almost $1.4 billion, in transfers from banks to partnerships set up by Enron, all reported by Enron as revenue from operations or investments. The money was purportedly used for the partnerships to buy Enron assets—assets that otherwise would have been difficult to sell. Using complex "total return swaps," Enron retained all rights to any profits from the purportedly sold asset—and also assumed responsibility for paying back the cash to banks, with interest. The deals, the *New York Times* concluded, provided "proof that participants may have been acting with a wink and a nod when providing loans disguised as sales."

■ Insiders Begin to See Writing on the Walls

By the time of the three-way money swap, more and more Enron insiders could see the writing on the wall. But the money was just too fabulous to do much about it.

For hitting 2000 stock price targets thanks to Fastow's pumped-up balance sheet, for instance, Enron's top two thousand people got $320 million—on top of their $432 million in bonuses and "special payments" the two previous years. The top hundred executives and traders shared more than $300 million of those funds—Fastow, more than $3 million; a key Fastow aide, $2.35 million; a third aide, $2.3 million; another, $1.55 million; another, $670,000.

But the really big money went to the men at the top: Kenneth Lay, Enron's founder, chairman, and alter ego, got $10.6 million, Chief Executive Jeffrey Skilling, $7.5 million. In addition, an influential West Coast gas trader got an $8 million bonus, $5.2 million went to a West Coast Power executive, $4.4 million to a West Coast gas desk executive, and $4.2 million to an Energy Services executive. But, as a special board committee later determined, executives had intentionally manipulated Enron's profits and stock price, inflating the profits by almost $1 billion through Fastow's byzantine partnership dealings.

"Everybody knew that money was coming and was hanging on for it," one former executive told the *New York Times,* something that lawyers representing Enron's lower-level workers (who suffered huge pension losses from Enron's stock freefall) called "powerful new evidence of potential fraud."

In addition to those bonuses, in the year before its bankruptcy filing, high-level Enron officials sold more than $1 billion in their company stock. Chairman Lay, personally and in family holdings, realized more than $100 million from sales in 2001 alone, on top of enormous profits on previously exercised options: $123.3 million in 2000, $43.8 million on 1999, and $13.1 million in 1998.

It is not unusual for corporate executives to sell their company stock—it is often the norm. But such sales combined with their delayed public reporting, while legal, had become quite controversial—and widespread in the early 2000s. Beyond Lay and Enron, for instance, fifteen executives at Colgate-Palmolive combined to sell $40 million in Colgate stock in 2000 and waited until the next year to report it. A retiring Procter & Gamble division president sold $2.8 million in company stock in mid-2001, but waited several months to report the sale. And two top executives of Tyco International, one then-CEO L. Dennis Kozlowski, sold more than $100 million in Tyco shares in late 2000 and 2001, but those sales did not become public for as long as a year—when Tyco stock was worth half what it had been at the time of the transactions. The same federal securities laws loophole that allowed the delayed reporting also allowed Enron's Lay to wait as long as thirteen months to disclose his own sales when the buyer was the company itself, enabling Lay to cash out many millions even as his company's stock plummeted.

At Enron's skyline-signature headquarters in Houston, some of the company's less jubilant—and less wealthy—executives were worrying about Fastow's partnerships, as were people from its outside auditing firm, Arthur Andersen. Since mid-1999, Enron had engaged in scores of transactions with the partnerships. It "sold" one a stake in a Brazilian power project, later "buying" it back. The same partnership "bought" a stake in any future gains on an Enron technology investment, a complex deal on which Enron actually declared a profit.

Decreasing a company's risk by moving holdings into separate partnerships that can then be sold to outside investors willing to assume those risks is not unusual in some businesses—especially entertainment and energy. But it was not until the late 1990s that Enron and other companies began pledging their own stock as a last-resort guarantee to investors who bought the partnership bonds. Investment bankers Citigroup, Credit Suisse First Boston, J. P. Morgan Chase, and Deutsche Banc Alex. Brown were so successful at helping Enron remove more than $8 billion in lagging assets from its balance sheet through such bond sales that the bankers took their newfound skill on the road, selling the concept to the El Paso Corporation, the Williams Companies, Columbia Natural Resources, Occidental Petroleum, and TXU Corporation, among others looking to appear more profitable.

The bankers worked with the companies to create the partnerships, then would sell big investors billions in the resulting partnership bonds—earning tens of millions in fees. At Enron, the process was refined into an art, making Enron seem much more profitable than it was. Some key executives seemed most interested in ensuring that the partnerships continually met critical accounting tests allowing them to be treated as separate tax entities rather than subsidiaries whose financial results would have to be shown on Enron's books.

From the start of these more aggressive partnerships, Enron's outside directors expressed concern and ordered the chief executive officer and other executives to closely monitor the Fastow partnerships. One Enron outside law firm later categorized the process as "haphazard" and said "important people involved in the procedures had limited grasp of their responsibilities." One of the executives charged with that oversight later characterized as "fairly cursory" his investigations on partnership transactions where employees in Enron's finance division—acting on behalf of Enron—were supposed to take positions against the direct financial interest of their boss—Fastow, according to the *New York Times.* One executive later shared his notes from the time in testimony to Congress, "Mr. Fastow wears two hats. . . . I find myself negotiating with Andy on Enron matters and am pressured to do a deal that I do not believe is in the best interests of the shareholders." A short time after penning this note, that executive was replaced as an officer—by another executive who, coincidentally, had invested $5,800 in one of the Fastow partnerships, only to see a return of $1 million just two months later.

"The haphazard nature of the approval process," for the partnerships, the *Times* began, "and the general disorganization of compliance procedures in the finance and accounting areas led to certain information being withheld—at least temporarily—from both the board and corporate filings." Routinely, Enron did not report details of partnership transactions in the quarter in which they occurred, but later, at best. And the bad news was often delayed or distorted in its eventual presentation, even to Enron's board.

■ Enron Thumbs Nose at California Energy Crisis

And Enron's creative approach to business wasn't limited to financial operations and reports. It became a sleight-of-hand business in itself.

Enron became the bad guy as Californians reeled from the frequent brownouts and big price hikes of an electric power crisis in 2000. Enron was charged with driving up energy prices through questionable investment techniques—and was charged with manipulating the esoteric energy-trading market to reap windfalls at consumers' expense.

Using strategies code-named "Fat Boy," "Ricochet," "Get Shorty," "Load Shift," and "Death Star," among others, Enron peaked its profits while adding to electricity costs and congestion on transmission lines. Death Star, for example, allowed Enron to be paid for "moving energy to relieve congestion without actually moving any energy or relieving any congestion." Load Shift allowed Enron to generate almost $30 million in profits in 2000 by using techniques that, according to documents, included creating "the appearance of congestion through the deliberate overstatement" of power to be delivered. In one strategy described in a December 2000 memo quoted by the *New York Times*, "Enron would buy power from a state-run exchange for $250 a megawatt-hour—the maximum under price caps—and resell it outside California for almost five times as much. State officials believe Enron and other power firms manipulated the state's market and played a crucial role in exacerbating the crisis, costing California consumers and utilities tens of billions of dollars in 2000 and 2001."

In a testament to insensitivity, Enron Chief Executive Skilling—discussing the situation in California at the time—asked a Las Vegas audience if they knew the difference between the state of California and the *Titanic*. Skilling stared at the audience and deadpanned: "At least when the *Titanic* went down, the lights were on," according to the *New York Times*. How appropriate that, in California nine days later to defend Enron's role, Skilling was hit in the face with a cream pie by a protester.

While proclaiming, "We are the good guys. We are on the side of the angels" in California, according to the *Times*, Skilling still maintained that his top priority was "to get the stock price up."

Boosting the stock price was critical because of the many Fastow partnerships that were financed, in effect, with Enron stock—deals that would fall apart if the stock price fell too low. One group of such partnerships kept $504 million in red ink off Enron's books by assuming the risks of future losses from Enron's portfolio of volatile technology stocks. But not long after tech stocks and the NASDAQ fizzled, so did Enron's own stock price, activating "trigger" provisions that would hurt Enron's credit rating and reported profits. As the sinking stock price got closer to those triggers, new and even more complex and fragile terms were negotiated with the partnerships, but an internal report later issued by Enron's board said the changes "were little more than a highly complex accounting construct that was designed to collapse."

The saga goes on and on. Enron executives started out in territory familiar to most executives. Wall Street rewards companies that produce consistent earnings growth. Executives whose companies don't, get fired. To avoid that, Enron found a legal way to not list some assets on its financial statements, massaging its profits in the process. To assure its growth, Enron began a bunch of new ventures—and needed a strong stock price to finance them, which meant it couldn't risk reporting lower profits or higher debts. And as one risky venture was leveraged on another, the bad news increased—as did the pressure to hide it, ethics and legality aside. Already comfortable with financial statements that didn't tell all, Enron took its giant step over the line.

And with its latest round of deals keeping $504 million in red ink off the books, Enron was able to report a profit of $425 million for the second quarter of 2001, another banner gain.

Some Enron executives rewarded their ingenuity by creating yet another partnership that they controlled, enabling them to sell their stake in a different partnership back to Enron for a $10 million profit. As if that weren't greed enough, one executive also sought—and miraculously got—another $2.6 million from Enron to cover his personal tax liability from the deal, a payout apparently approved by Fastow for one of his managing directors even after Enron's general counsel "unequivocally" advised against it. This, the board's special committee of directors later concluded, was "one of the most serious issues we identified."

But as Skilling basked publicly in the contrived earnings, Enron corporate lawyer Jordan Mintz worried about the Fastow partnerships, specifically the accuracy of their public descriptions and the rigor of internal oversight. Mintz wrote a confidential memo to Skilling, offering to discuss the situation at a time convenient for his boss. That time never came. Skilling resigned in August 2001 after just six months as chief executive—and sixty days after being proclaimed "the No. 1 CEO in the entire country."

■ Lay Returns to Save Enron's Sinking Ship

Skilling gone, legendary founder Ken Lay returned to the CEO role—and immediately appeared to open a dialogue with employees, primarily to pump them up. What Lay didn't expect was this:

"I am incredibly nervous that we will implode in a wave of accounting scandals," wrote a woman later identified as Sherron Watkins, an accountant who had been laid off the previous spring after eight years and rehired two months earlier to work for Fastow. "Skilling is resigning for 'personal reasons,' but I think he wasn't having fun, looked down the road and knew this stuff was unfixable and would rather abandon ship now than resign in shame in two years."

Lay and Enron General Counsel James Derrick Jr. wanted answers fast. They brought in the prestigious Houston law firm of Vinson & Elkins, which curiously had helped prepare some legal documents for some of the Fastow partnerships, according to the *New York Times*. Enron told the outside lawyers not to spend time examining accounting issues, even though that had been the heart of Watkins's warnings. The lawyers concluded Fastow's operation appeared to be on the level.

Watkins later told Congress she believed Lay was unaware of the severity of Enron's troubles—placing the blame for its ultimate demise on Skilling. She described a "culture of intimidation" inside the Skilling-run Enron, where no one felt confident enough to confront Skilling or Fastow. She said Fastow even tried to fire her after she signaled alarm in her note to Lay. She accused Skilling and Fastow of "duping Ken Lay and the board."

Referring to the more than $30 million Fastow reportedly made from the partnerships, Watkins was quoted by the *Times* as saying, "The saying around Enron was that, 'Heads, Mr. Fastow wins; tails, Enron loses.'" Watkins—nicknamed "Buzzsaw" for her outspokenness inside the company—said, "It was like staring at a time bomb."

Watkins's revelation made her something of a media star. Sam Donaldson introduced her to President Bush at the White House Correspondents' dinner in Washington. Dan Rather called from Afghanistan. She was cheered at a Court TV party in New Orleans. Her "whistleblower" persona brought movie deals and a $500,000 book advance. Diane Sawyer, Connie Chung, and Barbara Walters sent personal notes or called. People gawked as Watkins ate at restaurants, bursting into applause in one coffee shop. Even her church asked Watkins to speak—although that offer was rescinded by the Men's Ministry after a fellow church member who was also an Enron executive objected.

But Enron's efforts at deception went on.

Chung Wu was a respected broker at UBS Paine Webber in Houston, which had an exclusive agreement to handle Enron employee stock option and deferred benefit plans and also handled brokerage accounts for many executives and did substantial investment banking work for the company. So it was hardly appreciated that, while Lay was talking up Enron—predicting "a significantly higher stock price" on the same day he sold $4 million of his own stock back to the company, Wu was sending a message to clients warning that Enron's "financial situation is deteriorating" and they should "take some money off the table," according to the *New York Times*.

Enraged Enron executives weighed in with the power of the mighty and their business, with the leader of the stock option program sternly messaging Paine Webber officials: "Please handle this situation. This is extremely disturbing to me." Less than three hours later, yet another early warning of Enron's impending doom was silenced: Wu was fired. Paine Webber quickly disavowed and retracted his advice to clients, saying the stock—then trading at $36—was "likely heading higher than lower from here on out," categorizing the Enron stock as a "strong buy."

Times were tough. America had just endured the 9/11 terrorist attack on the World Trade Center in New York. And speculation was rampant in the wake of Skilling's abrupt departure. Lay tried to reassure his stunned workforce in e-mail and conversations, pledging that Enron was strong and that its stock—the bulk of the retirement plans for most—would recover.

While Lay was encouraging employees, Arthur Andersen auditors were discovering a mistake they had made a year earlier in Enron's books. That mistake—the method of accounting for the Enron stock used to finance some of Fastow's partnerships—had incorrectly added $1 billion to the assets on Enron's balance sheet. Correcting the error meant taking $1 billion in assets off Enron's balance sheet.

Meanwhile, Lay had decided to dismantle most of the Fastow partnerships. That would mean that investment losses masked for so long would have to be reported to shareholders. Worse, it would trim another $200 million from Enron's assets.

By October 2001, Enron announced its $1 billion deduction from third-quarter earnings to cover the irregularities, resulting in the company's first quarterly loss in four years. That bad news was followed by an even worse report, when the next morning's *Wall Street Journal* reported that $35 million in Enron's losses were related to its dealings with a pair of Fastow partnerships.

By the next week, Enron's stock price—which had been in the $30s—lost more than one-third of its value, falling to near $20 on Monday, October 22, 2001. The gotcha for Enron employees came when they couldn't sell their shares as the price plummeted because, "coincidentally," Enron was shifting the administration of its retirement plan and employee accounts were temporarily frozen. Symbolically, Fastow was placed on leave later that week, never to return to Enron. And—arguing that retaining top people to save the company was more important than ever—another $55 million in bonus payments went to key executives. Two traders in the reportedly successful energy-trading unit—whose profitability has since been called into question—each received cash bonuses of $8 million.

■ Searching for an Enron Savior

By now, Lay and his top aides were searching for a savior. The most willing was a cross-town competitor that had long resented Enron and its flashy ways, Dynegy Inc. But with its stock down to $15 and still falling, Enron was desperate. Lay's efforts to win help from Washington fell on deaf ears at the Commerce and

Treasury departments, despite Lay's longtime support of Republicans in general and President Bush in particular.

And troubles with Enron's auditors continued. Discussions between Enron and Andersen officials led to the conclusion that one Fastow partnership relied upon as independent for financial reporting did not actually meet requirements for such a designation.

In some other Fastow partnerships, ownership had been shifted away from independent investors—sometimes to Fastow and his financial executive colleagues, or even Enron itself—meaning that all of Enron's transactions with these partnerships had simply been transactions with itself. The Arthur Andersen auditors said hiding side deals between Fastow and his colleagues might have been a criminal act.

For J. Clifford Baxter, the former Enron vice chairman who had reportedly warned Skilling six months earlier, "We are headed for a train wreck and it's your job to get out in front of the train and try to stop it," the end was in sight. Baxter had "complained mightily" about the Fastow partnership deals to no avail. He even met with Skilling, who considered Baxter his best friend. Before Congress, Skilling said Baxter told him: "The thing that really gets me is it's like this: It's a beautiful day in Houston, Texas. You've got a hose. You're out watering your lawn. All your neighbors are outside talking. And suddenly the guy that lives next to you crashes out the door and says, 'I hear you're a child molester.' And then he turns back to his house and walks inside."

Baxter couldn't take the pressure—and the pain—any longer. Three days later, he committed suicide.

As the boards of Dynegy and Enron tentatively approved a merger, Enron was announcing that its storied financial performance for the last five years had been an illusion, created in part by Fastow's partnerships. Correcting the five years of improperly accounting for the partnership transactions meant $600 million in previously reported Enron profits were wiped out.

Meantime, Enron reassured Dynegy that its business was sound, with stock price problems stemming from the market panic triggered by Enron's latest news—a $1.2 billion equity reduction—only temporary. While Lay tried to hold the deal together, Enron was hemorrhaging cash, burning through $2 billion in just the week after it agreed to merge. Worse, according to the *New York Times,* Enron could not account for where a large portion of that money went. Enron also neglected to mention its huge cash outflow to Dynegy.

By November 19, the bottom dropped out. Enron filed a quarterly 10-Q revealing the cash drain and the requirement that Enron make accelerated payments on a note because of its troubles. Enron owed $690 million, payable within days. Not surprisingly, executives at Dynegy were furious. They had little advance warning of the filing. And, with the market in full-blown panic, Enron shares dropped from just above $9 to below the $7 floor on November 20. By the next week, Enron was rushing to settle the remaining merger issues when it heard the worst from Dynegy: The deal was off!

■ Bankruptcy and the Sorry Aftermath

Enron lawyers spent the next several days preparing its only remaining course—its bankruptcy filing. They worked early into the morning of December 2, ultimately filing in the Federal Bankruptcy Court in New York at 4:28 A.M.

Enron sought Chapter 11 protection from creditors while it reorganized, claiming assets of $49.8 billion and debts of $31.2 billion—plus the many losses and loans masked by the Fastow partnerships and not carried on Enron's balance sheet. It was the largest bankruptcy filing in U.S. history until that time, eclipsing Texaco's $35.9 billion 1987 filing. But its record would be short-lived—to be surpassed in less than a year by WorldCom's bankruptcy after similar shenanigans.

Enron's filing listed fifty pages of creditors, including some of America's largest banks—with Citibank and affiliates in first place, owed some $3 billion.

Thousands of Enron employees were laid off the next day, with little severance pay, having lost millions in their Enron retirement accounts.

But the Enron story was far from over. The aftermath shined a searchlight for any other corporations with similar misdeeds, suggesting they get their houses in order fast. It also sent shock waves from employees to suppliers, and even to investors.

One investor, in particular, got special attention: the Florida State Pension Fund. It may have lost more money than any other Enron investor—$328 million. To be sure, losing is a risk that's part of investing, but the unusual thing about the Florida Fund was that its investment advisory firm and the firm's star money manager were buying more and more Enron stock as its price continued to plunge. No other public pension fund incurred such a large loss, according to the *New York Times.*

The worse the news, the more investment guru Alfred Harrison bought for Florida. Even as Enron teetered on the brink just two weeks before filing bankruptcy, Harrison bought nearly 1.3 million more Enron shares, upping Florida's stake to 7.6 million Enron shares—a tiny position for Florida's $95 billion fund and the 650,000 government retirees whose pensions it is designed to pay, but a huge loss, nonetheless.

What caught the attention of Senate investigators and Florida's attorney general was an intriguing coincidence in Harrison's wrong-way bet on Florida's behalf: Frank Savage— an investment firm colleague and fellow board member of Harrison's—was also on the Enron board. Did Savage encourage the Florida Enron purchases? How else could an acknowledged investment wizard like Harrison have made such a bad call? Regulators wanted to know.

When Florida officials grilled Harrison about his relationship with Savage, Harrison claimed he did not know Savage was on the Enron board and rejected suggestions of outside influence, claiming that he, too, was a victim of Enron's misleading information. Though respected for his routine in-depth research, Harrison admitted buying Enron "on faith," according to the *New York Times*, even though its financial statements were a little "black boxy." Harrison concluded Enron "seemed to be on a deliberate path not to give full information," but still he bought. "Shame on me," he said later, "for not doing something."

Harrison's trademark was so-called "V" investing—buying companies whose shares had been beaten down, making money when they rose again. He had done it successfully with MBNA, Motorola, and Cisco Systems stock and made a large gain on Continental Airlines in the aftermath of the 9/11 tragedy. So why not Enron? Harrison began buying for the Florida Fund in November 2000, when the stock traded for about $80 a share, stepping up the pace throughout 2001. When Skilling quit as CEO, Harrison bought $26.1 million of Enron shares at about $36. Two months later, when Enron announced it had lost $1.2 billion from Fastow's side partnerships and that the Securities and Exchange Commission was investigating, Harrison bought $7.1 million more at $22. When Fastow was ousted as chief financial officer, Harrison bought $16.1 million more at prices from $16 to $12. In late October—when many analysts were downgrading Enron as its share price fell to $12—Harrison was saying Enron was worth $30 a share. And finally, when Enron announced in November 2001 that it had overstated profits earlier, Harrison bought $12.1 million more at $9. Harrison was still optimistic about prospects for an Enron-Dynegy merger and expressed his cautious belief in Enron to Florida officials just after Thanksgiving 2001. Then, one day later, Harrison sold all of Florida's 7.6 million Enron shares at a mere 28 cents per share.

Florida officials were furious about Harrison's apparent turnabout and overnight sale—made to the Lehman Brothers investment house in a private placement, the first time, Florida officials told the *New York Times*, that Florida Fund shares had been sold in a private placement. Worse, they said, Harrison did not tell Florida officials about the sale until after it was completed—an oversight that proved the last straw. "With that much to lose, you'd think they would pick up a phone and call someone," the Florida Fund's advisory board chairman told the *Times*. "It's one thing if it's a $100,000 loss, but we're talking $300 million here."

Harrison and his investment firm were fired by Florida the following week. In all, as Enron's largest shareholder in the quarter before its bankruptcy filing based on all its clients' holdings, Harrison's firm had lost more than $1 billion on all its clients' behalf in the Enron debacle.

■ Regulators Strike to Ensure "Never Again"

Federal investigators from numerous agencies and the Congress worked to piece together what happened—and what could be done to prevent a repeat performance in the future. Some Enron insiders cooperated with investigators. Most took the Fifth Amendment before Congress, except for the brazen former CEO Skilling, who proclaimed, "On the day I left, August 14, I believed the company was in strong financial condition. I wasn't there when it came unstuck." Skilling said he knew nothing of Enron's questionable practices. He found little support on Capitol Hill. Congressman Edward Markey, a Massachusetts Democrat, told Skilling: "You are employing the Sergeant Schultz defense of, 'I see nothing, I hear nothing,'" a reference to the character in the 1960s television series *Hogan's Heroes*.

As Enron's remaining directors stepped down in embarrassment for not having been diligent, it would be an understatement to call it too little, too late. For Enron's collapse also fractured a hard-won confidence built by two generations of a rigorous system of private disclosure and public oversight—a system that had given Americans confidence that they would not be fleeced, a system replicated the world over.

Enron was not the first big company to be felled by unscrupulous practices. In fact, well before the collapse, regulators and some professional investors worried that the system of oversight was breaking down. But the fact that a company as large and well-known as Enron could essentially vaporize in a matter of months shook even the most cynical on Wall Street.

Bad accounting was not why Enron failed, but it was the common thread across dozens of companies that had used accounting to inflate their profits or hide losses—either of which ultimately leads to the same ethical question. Too often, experts say, big company accounting was impenetrable or flat-out deceptive. Indeed, according to the *New York Times*, a 1998 survey of public company chief financial officers found that two-thirds had been asked by other executives to misrepresent company results—and 12 percent actually admitted succumbing. A 2001 study by Financial Executives International reported that public companies had revised their financial filings 464 times between 1998 and 2000—almost as many restatements as in the preceding twenty years.

Some of the world's best-known companies were suspected of using aggressive accounting to lift earnings, among them IBM and AOL Time Warner. A portfolio of blue chips would follow in the litany of suspected transgressors—Adelphia, Blue Light, Bristol Myers Squibb, Cendant, CMS Energy, Conseco, Deloitte, Dynegy, El Paso Energy, Ernst & Young, Global Crossing, Hanover Compressors, Merck, Merrill Lynch, Metromedia Fiber, Mirant, NCR, Network Associates, Peregrine Systems, Qwest, Reliant, Salomon Brothers, Tyco, Waste Management, Williams, WorldCom, Xerox—and even homemaking conglomerate Martha Stewart for "insider trading."

Intel's widely respected chairman turned author-philosopher, Andrew Grove, says he saw a "marked sentiment shift toward an unbridled exuberance—the values of a lot of people managing companies in this market environment drifted toward 'me, me, me.' I've been in business 40 years," Grove told the *Times*, "and I find myself feeling embarrassed and ashamed" to be a businessman.

■ Arthur Andersen Pays the Price

And a public reliant on transparency in public accounting was unforgiving. Arthur Andersen, an accounting firm once the "conscience of the industry," was caught in the middle of serious accounting miscues once too often at Enron.

On the heels of the Securities and Exchange Commission's filing civil fraud charges against an Andersen partner who apparently looked the other way on faulty reporting at Sunbeam and against Andersen itself for giving in to pressure from Waste Management, Enron's ultimate repudiation of financial statements certified by Andersen was the last straw. Enron had been one of Andersen's most prestigious clients, paying fees upwards of $50 million a year to Andersen for auditing and consulting.

Andersen defended itself, claiming that for four years it had categorized as "high risk" accounting judgments made in Enron's partnership accounting. A year before, according to the *New York Times*, Andersen partner David Duncan had told the Enron board's audit committee that his firm would approve Enron's financial statements without qualification, while warning that "close judgment calls on how to account for Enron's transactions with related parties . . . ran the risk of setting off close regulatory scrutiny."

That wasn't enough to save Andersen. In March 2002, in the first criminal charge ever brought against a major accounting firm, Andersen was indicted by a federal grand jury on a single count of obstruction of justice for destroying thousands of documents related to the Enron investigation. The indictment described a concerted effort by Andersen to shred records related to Enron in the auditor's offices in Houston, Chicago, and London, and in Portland, Oregon. Lawyers for Andersen said the wholesale shredding began October 23, 2001, in Houston—the day Andersen partners learned that the SEC would request Enron accounting records. Document destruction in Chicago began a month earlier. Federal officials were especially outraged that Andersen's Enron document destruction came just months after Andersen, as part of a settlement with the SEC in a Waste Management investigation, agreed not to commit future misdeeds.

"Andersen did not even appear contrite," the *New York Times* said. "There was no sense that the firm thought the Waste Management case showed it had a serious internal problem. The partners implicated in that case were not publicly disciplined—and one of them was even allowed to write the document-retention policy that David Duncan, the fired Houston partner in charge of the Enron audit, cited as support for the shredding he ordered. Had Andersen's management appeared to be vigilant about bringing change, perhaps the Justice Department would have been less eager to prosecute."

Instead, the SEC made it easy for the 20 percent of U.S. publicly traded companies that Andersen was auditing at the time to walk away, saying any companies that abandoned Andersen could file unaudited financials to meet current filing requirements and follow up with audited results—presumably from a new auditor—sixty days later.

"We are looking for a significant business hit," an Andersen spokesman said at the time—proving Andersen right about something. Within twenty-four hours, longtime clients and even some of its own foreign affiliates abandoned Andersen. Longtime and hometown loyalists Sara Lee, Abbott Laboratories, Northeast Utilities, and Brunswick joined the likes of Merck,

Delta, and FedEx in leaving Andersen. Foreign affiliates in Spain and Chile said they would sever ties to Andersen, and operations in Italy, Poland, Portugal, Switzerland, and other places followed suit—dooming any hopes for a sale that could save Andersen and its more than eighty-five thousand employees, virtually all people whose only sin was to be working honestly and diligently at the wrong firm at the wrong time.

Auditor Duncan would eventually plead guilty to a felony charge of obstruction of justice for shredding Enron documents—and agree to serve as a government witness in federal probes of both Enron and Andersen. And regulators, looking to avoid putting so much money on the line that it could ever again tempt auditors' conclusions, pushed legislation that would force accounting firms to separate their auditing and consulting functions in the future—a move opening floodgates of competition for consulting business. PricewaterhouseCoopers eventually spun off its consulting unit through a public stock offering, Deloitte Touche Tohmatsu separated Deloitte Consulting, and Ernst & Young and KPMG had already separated their consulting businesses. Big technology consulting companies such as EDS, IBM, and Accenture had the most to gain by directly entering the field.

The Fair Accounting Standards Board, the accounting rule maker in the United States, moved with uncharacteristic speed to enact rules that would require companies to include the results of their Enron-like partnerships in financial reports. For most companies, that will mean reporting significantly higher debt—and perhaps exceeding debt limits negotiated with their bondholders. The SEC also called for quicker and more comprehensive reporting of company finances, critical accounting decisions, and insider stock sales, which now must be reported within sixty days.

And, at every publicly traded company in America, by mid-2002 the CEO was required to personally certify the accuracy of the firm's financial results—and risk prosecution for future abuses.

That could not hold back the avalanche that started with Enron in Fall 2001 and became pervasive in the U.S. business climate then and beyond. In quick succession:

- WorldCom, the little Clinton, Mississippi, giant that rose from obscurity to acquire MCI for $30 billion, apparently looked profitable enough to be a David swallowing Goliath only because of its accounting irregularities. WorldCom sought bankruptcy protection in August 2002, after overstating previous earnings by more than $7 billion because of such accounting misstatements—adding that it would write off $50.6 billion as overstated value of sixty-five past acquisitions. CEO Bernard Ebbers, the onetime coach, milkman, and WorldCom folk hero who cashed out for $100 million-plus along the way, was, according to some, "out of his league in the rough-and-tumble world of telecommunications."
- The founder of Adelphia (one of the nation's largest cable companies), John Rigas, was arrested on charges of looting the company through corporate fraud and treating it with his family as a "personal piggy bank"—to the tune of more than $1 billion—to buy stock, build a private golf course, and safari in Africa.
- Samuel Waksal, founder of the biotechnology company ImClone Systems, was arrested at his Manhattan home and charged with insider stock trading.
- Conglomerate Tyco's former CEO, L. Dennis Kozlowski, was indicted on charges of evading more than $1 million in sales taxes on six paintings—worth tens of millions—bought by the company to hang in his home.
- Global Crossing, a telecommunications company, filed for bankruptcy protection after CEO Gary Winnick oversaw much of its decline—but not before he managed to sell $700 million of his own stock.

In the aftermath of it all, one living reminder of what happened in the early 2000s remained: the baseball park on the Houston skyline—home to the Houston Astros baseball team. It was "Enron Field." But after the business mess at Enron and beyond, the baseball club reclaimed its park—now "Astros Field."

Exercises in Ethics

A common theme in all the financial transgressions of Enron and others is the goal, usually deliberate, of deceiving others, primarily by issuing less than transparent financial reports that misrepresented what actually took place. The *New York Times* reported that two-thirds of chief financial officers surveyed in the late 1990s said they had been asked by company executives to misrepresent company results.

1. In your own business experience, what are the most significant transactions—current or historical—where similar "cloudy reporting" was tolerated or even encouraged in your company or industry?

_____

_____

_____

_____

_____

_____

2. List any transactions or activities within your company that might be less than arm's-length, as in Enron's early days (when oversight and disclosure were strong), and about which you and your board must remain constantly vigilant to ensure total transparency.

_____

_____

_____

_____

_____

_____

3. Analyze whether and why the value of that less-than-arm's-length business justifies the temptation and potential risk it may pose to your company.

_____

_____

_____

_____

_____

_____

_____

4. What are the salient "teachable" lessons on business ethics that you can extract from these examples to use in your Teachable Point of View to teach and provide examples to employees on your company's position on business ethics?

_____

_____

_____

_____

_____

_____

_____

5. How will whatever safeguards your company has in place ensure that people are not gradually tempted to cross the line and provide misleading or concocted results?

_____

_____

_____

_____

_____

_____

_____

2

Ethics and Culture of ServiceMaster Sustain Important Values Over Time

C. William Pollard

Chairman Emeritus
ServiceMaster Inc.

Editors' Note: ServiceMaster is a living example of a value-driven organization, one where profits are not paramount, but where they are expected to come as a result of the ethical treatment of customers, employees, suppliers, and other constituents. The "oddball" company's former chairman describes its roots and values.

We are delighted to partner with the University of Michigan Business School on this important event, the eighth in a series sponsored by the ServiceMaster Foundation. Previous events have been held at the Drucker School at Claremont, Northwestern, Notre Dame, Harvard, Oxford, Yale, and the University of Southern California. And we are delighted to add Michigan to that impressive list.

This series is designed to honor the work and memory of Ken Hansen and Ken Wessner, both of whom served as CEOs of ServiceMaster and played important roles in developing and leading our company and in establishing the values and culture of our business. For them, the business firm was not simply an economic entity to maximize profits but was also a vehicle for the development and growth of people as they served customers and produced results. They encouraged the growth of a community where the whole person could flourish and grow—where the physical, rational, and yes, even spiritual self could be nourished—and a community where every person, regardless of difference, would be treated with dignity and worth.

This view has become an integral part of the theory of our firm and the way we run our business. We recognize, however, that this process of implementing values is never over and is al-

Delivered at the Hansen-Wessner Memorial Lecture, April 12, 2002, at the University of Michigan Business School, Ann Arbor, Michigan. Copyright 2002, ServiceMaster Foundation. Reprinted with permission. All rights reserved.

ways being challenged. As we sponsor this series, our purpose is to continue to learn and improve as we ask the basic question:

Can the business firm not only excel at generating profits and creating value for its shareholders and customers but also become a moral community for the development of human character and the nourishment of the spiritual side of one's humanity?

When ServiceMaster raised this question more than twenty-five years ago, we were in the minority. Today, issues like the source of moral authority and spirituality in the workplace are popular topics. Numerous books have been written about the subject, and feature articles in *Fortune, Forbes, BusinessWeek,* and the *Wall Street Journal* have discussed the subject of spirituality in the workplace and the need for moral and ethical standards in the workplace.

Just this week I spent two days with Steven Carter, a noted legal authority from Yale, consulting with ten CEOs of public and private companies—large firms asking the question, "Is it possible to have a firm that is inclusive and also faith-friendly?"

Last night I shared the platform with the dean at a student-convened symposium at the Harvard Business School where the principal issue discussed was the role of spirituality in the workplace.

So the issue of ethics—the practice of right behavior and the source of what's right and wrong—is a relevant issue, not only because of the Enrons of the world but also because it is a part of who we are and how we work together.

Today we have the opportunity to focus on this issue with a wise and experienced presenter and several learned respondents.

I especially want to thank Secretary Baker for taking time out of his busy schedule to be here. Jim will not only give a fine presentation, but the values he speaks of are the values he lives by—both in his personal life and public life.

□

Exercises in Ethics

ServiceMaster seeks more than profits. It places great importance on the development and growth of its employees on three dimensions—physical, rational, and spiritual.

1. What are some of the things your firm provides to help employees flourish and grow on those dimensions? And what are some of the things your company could provide to encourage better growth of the "total person" among employees?

	Provide Now	*Could Provide*
a. Physical	■ _____	■ _____
	■ _____	■ _____
	■ _____	■ _____
b. Rational	■ _____	■ _____
	■ _____	■ _____
	■ _____	■ _____
c. Spiritual	■ _____	■ _____
	■ _____	■ _____
	■ _____	■ _____

2. Develop your own business rationale for providing these opportunities for the personal growth of employees—and how it provides value to the company—to incorporate into your Teachable Point of View on business ethics.

_____

_____

_____

_____

_____

3

Sustaining Business Ethics Requires Teachable Point of View

Jonathan Ward

Chairman and Chief Executive Officer
ServiceMaster Inc.

Editors' Note: Developing a Teachable Point of View is a critical step for any leader, but especially when essential topics such as ethics in business must be demonstrated and communicated to an organization. Jon Ward introduces former Secretary of State James Baker III as an exemplar of a leader who has this ability to learn, reflect, and teach.

L ife is about building your Teachable Point of View and then taking action on it.

That could not be more important or timely.

For the last several months, headlines and editorial pages have been filled with facts, speculation, and recommendations about the topic of business ethics—people, personal ethics, legal obligations, moral responsibilities. They all come together.

It is my pleasure to introduce Secretary James Baker.

Last night I had the chance to see Paul McCartney, who is now sixty, and Secretary Baker—we won't tell your age, but it is north of seventy. Whatever you do in politics and whatever McCartney's doing in entertainment is a heck of a lot better than we business executives—who look pretty beaten up by the time we get to be fifty!

Jim Baker has a long and distinguished career of service. He served in senior government positions under three U.S. presidents. Under Gerald Ford, he served as Undersecretary of Commerce. Under President Ronald Reagan, he served as Secretary of the Treasury, chairman of the President's Economic Policy Council, and White House chief of staff. Under President George Bush, he served as Secretary of State, White House chief of staff, and senior counselor to the president.

Delivered at the Hansen-Wessner Memorial Lecture, April 12, 2002, at the University of Michigan Business School, Ann Arbor, Michigan. Copyright 2002, ServiceMaster Foundation. Reprinted with permission. All rights reserved.

Jim Baker is an active leader in American presidential politics. We all saw that in 2000. He led presidential campaigns for Ford, Reagan, and Bush over five consecutive presidential elections. Mr. Baker received the Presidential Medal of Freedom in 1991—and has been a recipient of many other awards for public service and numerous honorary degrees.

Presently Mr. Baker is a senior partner in the law firm of Baker and Botts and senior counselor to the Carlisle Group, a merchant banking group located in Washington, D.C.

Jim and his wife, Susan, currently reside in his hometown of Houston. They have eight children and fourteen grandchildren.

Jim is known for his insight, his intelligence, and his ability to turn thinking into action.

Today's news offers fertile ground for skepticism and doubt. At the same time, it offers us all an opportunity to sharpen our own thinking, to refine our own Teachable Points of View on leadership, on both business and public service, and to bring the moral dimension to all we do in our work.

We can all benefit from more debate and reflection on capitalism, ethics, and human nature. Jim Baker is both a wise observer and an active participant on the issue of business ethics in skeptical times.

Exercises in Ethics

Take a first cut at identifying the key elements that will be incorporated into your Teachable Point of View on business ethics.

1. Ideas:

_____

_____

_____

_____

_____

_____

2. Values:

_____
_____
_____
_____
_____
_____
_____
_____
_____

3. Energy:

_____
_____
_____
_____
_____
_____
_____
_____

4. Edge:

_____
_____
_____
_____
_____
_____
_____
_____

Business Ethics in Skeptical Times

James A. Baker III
61st U.S. Secretary of State

□

Editors' Note: Free markets and free people in the post–cold war era are not that different—both thriving with freedom to do great things and achieve incredible results. In both cases, however, Secretary Baker describes the inevitable human tendency to cross the line and go too far, whether by premeditation or accident. The important thing, Baker argues, is for society not to be swept up in the mania of the moment and overreact to transgressions from Enron to Watergate, rushing to enact regulations we'll later regret. Leadership requires both patience in time and perspective and an overriding belief that free markets— like free societies—are both ethical and self-correcting. In the end, public prudence and skepticism form an essential counterbalance that ultimately drives the pace of change—whether through fallen presidents, tougher laws, or public shame. That, Baker says, is the promise and price of freedom.

I am not a theorist, always being more inclined toward practicalities than reflection—what people in Washington call a "pragmatist." To some, that's a dirty word. To me, it's not, as long as you're a principled pragmatist—because it doesn't do any good to have the greatest ideas in the world if you can't put them into action.

But that action must always be principled. And sometimes it is not. It is with some sadness to me that the most prominent business failure of recent times is Enron. This is a Houston story—and Houston is my home. I've seen a lot of people harmed by what happened—employees, investors, creditors, companies that did business with Enron. This event has cast a

Delivered at the Hansen-Wessner Memorial Lecture, April 12, 2002, at the University of Michigan Business School, Ann Arbor, Michigan. Copyright 2002, ServiceMaster Foundation. Reprinted with permission. All rights reserved.

shadow over our entire system of free-market capitalism. And that's another cause for regret.

I am also saddened for personal reasons. I know many board members and officers of Enron. Some are friends. I very much doubt that my friends set out one morning with the objective of misleading anybody and started planning a major conspiracy to mislead and injure the public. Yet, however good their intentions, decisions were made about business, accounting, and disclosure matters that cannot be justified. Each bad decision begot another. In the end, the financial community understandably lost confidence—and Enron collapsed. I can't remember a business failure in the United States that happened with such rapidity from start to total collapse.

This is not the first time we've had to ask, "What went wrong?" And those of us who are realists know it won't be the last. So long as fallible human beings are in charge, we can expect more businesses to fail, generally through bad luck or bad judgment, but sometimes through negligence, malfeasance, or even active criminal misbehavior. Enron is another reminder that we live in an imperfect world where bad things happen. Recall the savings and loan mess, a $260 million bailout. We put the fox in charge of the henhouse, with, in effect, savings and loan executives or former executives regulating the savings and loan industry.

I serve on the boards of two corporations listed on the New York Stock Exchange, one unlisted corporation, and two large nonprofit corporations. So while it is true that I am now retired from government, I have not retired from governance. Indeed, I see many similarities between my duties as a public servant and my duties now as a director, both of which were and are intertwined with the most profound issues of ethical conduct.

The challenge our society faces today is to study events like Enron and take lessons from them about ethical conduct—personally, as representatives of our companies, and as public policymakers.

What should I do differently? What should my company do differently? What should our system of free market capitalism do differently?

In seeking these answers, I will touch on four general topics:

- All times are skeptical times.
- Free market capitalism is an ethical system.
- First, do no harm.
- What we can do.

■ All Times Are Skeptical Times

Enron, understandably, has triggered public skepticism. But we need to maintain our perspective. For business, all times are skeptical times or should be skeptical times. The ultimate form of skepticism was called Marxism. It was a system of government and economics based on the premises that capitalism abuses workers and that central planners can do better. Of course, Marxism has failed and the thing it opposed—capitalism—has won. Capitalism survived because it works and because, on balance, it treats everyone, including workers, better than any alternative. Or, to revise Winston Churchill's famous statement: *Many forms of economy have been tried in this world of sin and woe. No one pretends that a market economy is perfect or all wise. Indeed, it has been said that a free market is the worst form of economy, except all those other forms that have been tried from time to time.*

Thus inherent within capitalism, we find skepticism. Theodore Roosevelt complained about "malefactors of great wealth" and started the antitrust movement—a very good thing. Franklin Roosevelt blamed the Great Depression on "economic royalists"—although I'm not sure that's true. Eisenhower warned about the "military-industrial complex." And don't forget that Vice President Al Gore won more than 48 percent of the popular vote in November 2000 with a promise to stand up to the "powerful forces" in our economy. Add the 2.74 percent won by Ralph Nader and you can argue that a majority of Americans support some form of economic populism, a philosophy my old boss, Ronald Reagan, might have described like this: "If it moves, tax it. If it keeps moving, regulate it. And if it stops moving, subsidize it."

Enron fell on fertile soil, a reminder of why skepticism is an essential element of both a healthy market economy and a mature ethical perspective. Our system is built on both. It is impossible to have a market economy without the rule of law, as the problems of Russia exemplify. They really want a market economy, but haven't yet understood that the basics must be in place first, particularly a system of laws. Private property, enforceable contracts, corporations, stocks, bonds, courts, banks—they are all creatures of law, and we cannot do business without them. We can argue about the details—particularly overly complex laws and regulations that govern business competition, labor, securities, the environment, and taxes—but the principle is inarguable: The rule of law is a necessary and desirable precondition to a functional market economy.

And what is the rule of law? It is institutionalized skepticism about human nature. With the rule of law, Blackacre (a fictional property often used to illustrate legal examples) changes hands through voluntary sales and through inheritance. Without the rule of law, Blackacre goes to the neighborhood bully.

Likewise, the conduct of business requires prudent skepticism, whether as an investor, employee, officer, or board member. Skepticism is a critical business skill. In a business acquisition, for example, it is formalized in "due diligence," the buyer's investigation of the company or assets to be acquired. In the old days, we checked the horse's teeth. Today, we kick the tires. In both cases, we're acting with a healthy degree of skepticism. One problem at Enron, in retrospect, is that at critical points in the company's history, either there was not enough skepticism or there was no skepticism at all.

The rule of law, ordinary commercial prudence, and the impulse to act ethically in business all reflect a healthy skepticism about human nature. As a moralist, I certainly do not agree that greed is good. But as a realist, I understand that greed *is*— it exists.

■ Free Market Capitalism Is an Ethical System

Free-market capitalism is, itself, an ethical system. The genius of capitalism is to pacify a destructive human characteristic— greed—into benign self-interest, something we call "incentive."

It's hard to improve on Adam Smith's explanation: "It is not from the benevolence of the butcher, the brewer, or the baker, that we expect our dinner, but from their regard to their own interest." Under this system, Smith wrote, "Every man, as long as he does not violate the laws of justice, is left perfectly free to pursue his own interest in his own way, and to bring both his industry and capital into competition with those of any other man."

The Wealth of Nations was published in 1776, the same year as the Declaration of Independence. *The Wealth of Nations* established the theoretical foundation for the free market. The Declaration of Independence set the American colonies on a path toward the form of republican democracy established a few years later under our Constitution. Both free-enterprise capitalism and republican democracy have succeeded beyond measure.

One of the strengths of our system is that we believe in doing business ethically and we believe in conducting our international politics ethically. This can put us at a great disadvantage in securing contracts in other countries because paying people off is against U.S. law. I hear all the time from clients of my law firm looking for representation overseas, trying to get a fair shake to acquire a contract, about Country X coming in, slipping some minister something, and we're out of business. It's sad, but it happens.

We must also understand that we'll never be able to impose our system on others—and we probably ought not to try. And, sometimes, this, too, can put us at a disadvantage. In international politics, you sometimes do business with people who are not too savory. We're doing it today. You can't wage a war on terrorism without fighting it down-and-dirty—because you're fighting people who are down-and-dirty. For years, we jumped all over our human intelligence capabilities. We made the CIA get out of the human intelligence business because it was dirty and the people were unsavory. Hopefully, we're back into the human intelligence business—however dirty—because when you're engaged in a war on terrorism, you had better be deeply involved. At the same time, we try hard—every chance we get—to impress upon other countries that democracy, free markets, the rule of law, freedom of the individual, respect for religion, and a free press are what it's all about—and we've had a lot of success.

As Secretary of State of this wonderful country at almost the best time anybody could have been, I saw communism collapse, the Berlin Wall fall, the cold war end. Everybody wanted to get close to the United States and embrace democracy and the free market, save one or two little dictatorships sprinkled around the globe.

As James Madison wrote in Federalist No. 51: "What is government itself, but the greatest of all reflections on human nature? If men were angels, no government would be necessary." The American form of government is not perfect. Among other things, it failed to prevent the Civil War. On balance, however, it has worked marvelously. Consider the painful case of Watergate. President Nixon violated our trust, abused the power of his office, and challenged the rule of law. But the true legacy of Watergate is that our system identified and peacefully expelled an unethical president—an event in many ways unprecedented in human history. Our free press did its job exposing the wrongdoing, the impeachment machinery cranked up, and President Nixon resigned.

After Watergate, people demanded higher standards. And we had four presidents in a row with the very highest character. President Gerald Ford—as I don't need to remind people at Michigan—was one of the finest men ever to serve as president. He restored honor to the Oval Office. Jimmy Carter, in my view, was wrong on many policies and perhaps less skilled at governance, but nobody would ever question his honesty. I certainly never would. And Ronald Reagan and George H. W. Bush were both men of the highest integrity.

Watergate, like Enron, was an ethical failure. Like Enron, it created great skepticism about the system. But it is wrong to see Watergate *solely* as a failure of our system. In fact, it demonstrated the genius of our founders and the strength of the ethical system they created.

■ First, Do No Harm

We must take great care that, in our eagerness to avoid another Enron, we do not seek reforms that are inconsistent with the ethical structure of our economic system or that weaken it. Or, put another way, the proper response to Enron is not a simple-minded rush to "do something," with little concern about what that something might be. Instead, the first concern of the business ethicist, like the doctor, should be to do no harm.

The myth of Watergate—that politics is essentially corrupt and that "everybody does it"—inspired two very fundamental changes in our system of governance. One was the enactment of unrealistic and deeply flawed campaign finance laws. We've now seen how deeply flawed they were and have enacted some legislation correcting some of the problems. The other miscue was creating the independent counsel's office.

On campaign finance laws, columnist Robert Samuelson wrote: "In the futile effort to regulate politics, the 'reformers' "— Samuelson puts that term in quotation marks to signal his scorn—"have manufactured most of the immorality, illegality and cynicism they deplore."

The right answer—consistent with the Constitution and the ethical structure of our system of government—is not to criminalize our politics, thereby politicizing our criminal justice system, but to require full and immediate disclosure of all campaign contributions, with severe penalties for those who fail to report or who file erroneous or misleading reports. This is the political analogue to the honest disclosures that should be required in the world of corporate finance.

As for independent federal prosecutors, the consensus today—no matter your party, even among those who originally supported the commissioning of these Lone Rangers to clear up an allegedly corrupt system—is that the cure proved far worse than the disease. These prosecutors were not subject to the checks and balances the founders built into our system. Countless investigations produced very little evidence of smoke and even less of fire, but at the cost of further weakening public confidence in the system and creating skepticism where none was justified. I have always opposed the independent counsel law. But while it was the law, the executive branch was absolutely obligated to cooperate with all investigations, and the presidents I served did just that. I can't tell you, though, how many countless hours we spent being interviewed by the FBI, testifying on one thing or another, because under the independent counsel statute if you were a high enough government official, all that was required was a mere allegation that you did something wrong. That resulted in the appointment of an independent prosecutor.

I have the same concerns about our response to Enron. We need to understand that our economy, just like our political system, is self-correcting. Or, as one *Financial Times* article proclaimed in its headline, "Capitalism Will Clean Itself Up." We've just been through this with the political system—and we don't need to make the same mistake with our economy and business system. Enron and its leaders have been punished and will be further punished in the future, justifiably so. And it has already been pretty harsh when you think about all the reputations and lawsuits they must defend. The collateral damage to employees, creditors, and other companies should not be minimized. But we also should not exaggerate the impact of Enron's failure on our system. To my knowledge, not one home or business lost electricity or natural gas as a result of the failure, nor was there significant turmoil in the markets for those commodities. In addition, justified market skepticism swept through our economy on a search-and-destroy mission against dishonest accounts and misleading disclosures. And there is little doubt that Enron will stimulate useful reforms in our generally accepted accounting principles and, more important, in our generally accepted business principles.

Any corporate director will tell you the process is under way. I have seen it from the inside—and it has operated with stunning efficiency. Every major company today has an ethics code, and some have provisions in that code that even talk about the importance of coming forward any time you see something going on that you don't like. Still, people must be willing to cross the boss. It gets back to hiring the right type of people. From experience, I can tell you that the most valuable adviser to the president of the United States is an adviser who is willing to tell him the truth. It is really easy to be a yes-man to the president.

I don't think I am a Pollyanna. I do not disregard or excuse the harm done by Enron or the weaknesses it exposed in our system. It did a lot of harm to a lot of innocent people, and exposed some very serious weaknesses. What I urge, instead, is that we evaluate that harm and those weaknesses in the proper context—consider whether we agree that our market is, itself, an ethical system, that it is self-correcting in response to the failure of Enron, and that further reforms should be designed to strengthen that ethical system—not weaken it. A danger even greater than doing nothing would be if economic populists were able to use Enron as an excuse to legalize issues that, frankly, should be left to the companies and the market. Or, in Reagan's words: "If it keeps moving, regulate it."

■ What We Can Do

How can we review our own conduct and the conduct of our companies to strengthen them against the virus that infected Enron?

For starters, I warn my fellow directors that we all must treat the de jure reality of our jobs as the de facto reality. Most boards are self-perpetuating and CEOs recruit most directors. Despite that, we should never forget that we all represent the shareholders—with a particular burden falling on outside directors, who should be truly independent. This is not only a legal obligation, it is a moral obligation. And we simply cannot do that job properly unless we are willing, from the first day on the job, to cross management if it is necessary. You cannot serve effectively as a director of any corporation unless you are willing to tell it like it is—and that will oftentimes mean crossing management.

Independence is no good, however, unless the outside directors know what they are doing. In fact, it could be bad if you didn't know what you were doing! While professional qualifications may differ from case to case, being a good director always demands education, experience, and maturity. It also demands courage—perhaps most important of all. As I said, it's not easy to cross management, particularly if you are relying on that directorship for whatever it might be—financial rewards, status, or whatever—because when you cross them, oftentimes it means you better be ready to tell them, "Either you do this, or I'm out of here." And that certainly demands courage.

Directors should also limit their number of board memberships. The job today is harder than a few years ago. We cannot meet the demands of that job if our attention is divided in too many ways.

We also need to take another look at our system of executive compensation and reevaluate it. Frankly, we are paying some executives too much, and we are doing it in ways that create perverse incentives. Stock options have been the subject of much discussion and they may have their place. But options are truly exposed as a hoax when they are repriced again and again to guarantee that they can be exercised. They are also dangerous when they tempt executives to make questionable accounting and reporting decisions, "just this once," to lift their options above water. We must look for better ways to tie our executives' compensation to the long-term success of our companies, not quarterly results. This is tough. And the demand for short-term results in our system today is a difficult problem that we need to examine in depth.

We should also be alert to accounting and reporting decisions that follow the letter of the law but violate the spirit of the law. Accounting rules today are so esoteric and difficult to understand that you might be literally within the legal constraints of a particular rule—but way outside its spirit. The temptation is strong, but it must be resisted. The ultimate ethical value here is simple honesty. It may cost a few points in the stock price today, but it is the right thing to do—and, in the long run, the market rewards honesty and credibility. Remember, too, that ever-more-complex regulation sometimes encourages ethical corner cutting by suggesting that legalistic compliance is ethically sufficient—the moral hazard of overregulation.

In the end, in business as in politics, credibility is hard to acquire, but very easy to lose.

■ Conclusion

There is no substitute for electing men and women of character and integrity to our boards and executive suites. This is not inconsistent with the idea that free-market capitalism is an ethical system. Our founders understood that public virtue was absolutely essential. "Of all the dispositions and habits which lead to political prosperity," George Washington said in his Farewell Address, "religion and morality are indispensable supports."

As we consider the moral and ethical framework of the marketplace, we would do well to remember Washington and realize that the best business firms are not simply economic entities that maximize profits but also vehicles for the development and growth of people, their firms, and the customers and communities they serve—the very vision of ethical government and ethical markets at work.

Exercises in Ethics

Jim Baker asks three pressing questions that every businessperson must be able to answer in the post-Enron environment. Answer them for your own firm:

1. In the wake of Enron,

   a. What should I do differently?

   _____

   _____

   _____

   _____

b. What should my company do differently?

_____

_____

_____

_____

c. What should our system of free market capitalism do differently?

_____

_____

_____

_____

2. Building on Baker's biggest point for action, analyze your board of directors, listing very candidly the names of those board members who are

a. Truly independent:

_____

_____

_____

_____

_____

b. Who are also well-qualified, by the following criteria:
   Education:

_____

_____

   Experience:

_____

_____

   Maturity:

_____

_____

_____

c. Who also have the freedom
and courage to challenge
management:

_____
_____
_____
_____

d. Who also serve on no
more than two or three
other boards:

_____
_____
_____
_____

3. Are the directors whose names remain after these questions the right
number and right individuals to be the primary outside enforcers of
your company's ethical standards? If not, how can you improve the
composition of your board to improve its oversight capability?

_____
_____
_____
_____
_____
_____
_____

4. Incorporate the importance of the oversight role of directors and
your actions to enhance it into your Teachable Point of View on
business ethics.

_____
_____
_____
_____
_____
_____
_____

5

Peripheral Issues Can Evolve; "Core Ethics" Must Be Stable

C. K. Prahalad

*Professor of Corporate Strategy
and International Business
University of Michigan Business School*

Editors' Note: Norms may evolve with the times, but every leader and business must have "core invariants"—those ethics and values that have stood the test of time and are not flexible. Understanding these absolutes and contrasting them with those values that may be more flexible—is critical to maintaining a society that experiments and takes risks at the margin, while retaining its ethical base.

approach this task with great humility, because business ethics is a very complex topic.

Let me put in perspective where I come from. I wear two hats. First, for twenty-three years, I was a full-time professor here at Michigan—and I still am. And that gives me a sense of perspective from the large companies that I study. I am also on two large boards, on the board of a large nongovernmental organization (NGO) that operates around the world, and I'm chairman of a small start-up. That diversity provides a very different perspective—going from a very small start-up to the most established names in American industry.

I've been thinking about this topic for the last couple of years, and I believe we have to go to the field constantly, because the field is critical to informed theory. But I also believe that good theory can inform practice.

I'll start by reflecting on the four critical points raised by Secretary Baker. They're all terribly important.

The first one—skepticism—is a critical element of our system. That's a fundamental starting point. Second—the rule of law—it's a precondition for markets to function. Third—can reforms overcorrect? And finally—how do we deal with an Enron-type scandal?

Delivered at the Hansen-Wessner Memorial Lecture, April 12, 2002, at the University of Michigan Business School, Ann Arbor, Michigan.

■ Skepticism Provides Checks and Balances

Skepticism really means checks and balances. You can wonder whether it's just a play on words, but I believe not. Checks and balances are required when we explicitly recognize that in our economy and society there are competing interests, and they must be explicitly balanced. Tension is always inherent in the system—and that is what makes the system vibrant.

If we ever destroy that vibrant quality, we destroy the system.

Sometimes the system will get out of balance because of the very nature of tension. Therefore, there is always skepticism of the moment. That's what we are seeing after Enron—a skepticism of the moment, not a fundamental disagreement with the system itself. It simply must be brought back in balance.

The momentarily convenient desire to eliminate the tension between those checks and balances would result in inefficiencies. But in sticking with the system, we must expect certain things because they are part of the checks and balances—such as the fundamental right, in a large company, to the legitimacy of dissent. This legitimacy of dissent is not only a fundamental principle for our economy and a basic right in our society but an essential check and balance—and I wish more companies understood that this legitimacy of dissent is critical to their internal due process, to providing share-of-voice, and to creating structural impediments to the excesses that can come from concentration of power.

When companies fail, they do so because they have—much earlier—destroyed these structural impediments to the concentration of power. It may be frustrating to deal in a system where dissent is legitimate, but it's worth it. More important, how many managers recognize that they operate in a system that needs these checks and balances, however frustrating?

The board of directors is another structural impediment that legitimizes dissent. And, as a board member, that is what I see my role to be—presenting an alternate perspective on some issues. Auditors are another mechanism that should provide checks and balances. And consumers are joining in a very active fashion—aided by the Internet—to create activist consumer groups to provide checks and balances to the excesses of companies.

To fulfill the role of providing a healthy skepticism as a board member, my job is to challenge the CEO and senior managers on key issues. In doing that, I must distinguish between matters of principle and projects of large size, which require very different types of due diligence.

■ The Rule of Law and Overcorrection

On the rule of law as a precondition for efficient markets, look at why the two East India companies—the Dutch East India Company and the British East India Company—had such differential success.

The Dutch East India Company got a hundred-year charter from the king. It had a built-in end game. So merchants were extraordinarily successful for the first sixty or seventy years, and then they spent all the money building their palaces in Amsterdam.

The British East India Company had a very successful start because the British invented the joint-stock company, where you can hold title in perpetuity and pass it on generation after generation. Those property rights, going back two hundred or three hundred years, have been fundamental to creating the vibrant global economy we know today.

Can reforms overcorrect?

They will—and they should.

Overcorrection is a result of not knowing exactly what the correct balance is. If you overcorrect, as with the swing of a pendulum, you can always change and reduce the dysfunctional extreme of the correction. But if you do not correct enough, it's hard to know if your response was appropriate.

So we will overcorrect after Enron—and I'm not overly worried, because in the short term it may create a problem, but from a ten-year perspective, we will recorrect.

Trial and error in improving the system is the sibling of checks and balances in our society. Trial and error is how we build consensus, experiment, and improve.

■ Reacting to the Enron Situation

So how should we react to Enron?

It is not just Enron. We have Tyco, Xerox, Qwest, and many others. And we are going to continue to see a wide variety of firms under government scrutiny. A large number of options repricing schemes have been unearthed—and there will be more. Enron just happened to be the lead player.

Why is this happening now?

All the dramatic disclosures—one more annoying and damaging than the next—have their roots in three basic causes:

- First, the complexity of business itself, complicated by the peculiarities within individual companies and industries.
- Second, the inherent limitations of current checks and balances.
- Third, the violations of ethical guideposts that stem from personal values and experiences—and no system can solve that problem.

Complexity: It is very common today to have a global corporation that operates in a hundred countries with twenty businesses, plus being involved in fifty to a hundred separate partnerships and alliances. The number of transactions—both routine and unique—can boggle the mind. No single person can understand and manage the details of the entire organization. Senior managers and the board must depend on systems, culture, and the senior management team to enforce the appropriate controls.

Even then, this is not so straightforward. A few specific examples:

First, what is the process for revenue recognition in multi-year software contracts and projects in a global economy? This is a very complex accounting problem. But, beyond that, should the Japanese subsidiary follow the U.S. parent's standards? When this came up in a board meeting, the CEO took a very strong view: "Japan will follow American standards because we are an American company." I said, "We'll lose some business." He said, "So be it." It was not easy to push down the throats of managers from the Asia operation, but the good news is, we didn't lose any business.

Second, how dependent are managers on uniform systems around the world? What if we have twenty-five legacy systems with different approaches to revenue recognition that came with various acquisitions? IT experts and people who understand how systems work know that this is a huge problem. How do we ensure quality? What do we audit? Transactions, systems, or both? Where are the latent risks? Does the competition for talent and low-cost capital drive managers to create incentives that are dysfunctional?

Third, do you use Napster to download music? This question requires some truth and candor.

Do you know it's illegal?

■ **The Lure of Napster**

You mean you didn't know you could not take the intellectual property of others and just download it?

Fourteen million young men and women download music, and most of the time, when I ask senior managers this question, they say, "But I don't do it . . . my son does it for me."

There is an important idea here that we need to understand: Ethical concerns evolve. Fourteen million young people are saying, given the new technology, we ought to revisit the meaning of property—whether movies, music, or whatever.

It is premature to know where these new Internet-forced ethical dilemmas will take us, or what new ethical dilemmas stem cell research and changes in biotechnology will create. So whether Napster is ethical is interesting, but a more interesting issue is how we think about privacy and what role Napster should have in ensuring that privacy.

This list may appear random, starting from accounting for multi-year contracts and winding up in stem cell research, but it is not. These represent distinctly different types of ethical dilemmas.

■ Developing an Ethical Framework

Here's a simple framework to help think about how an ethical framework can be built inside a company.

Imagine a hard core at the center that does not change with time, context, circumstance, or business demand. These are values that have stood the test of time: Integrity, personal accountability, due process, respect for the individual, property rights, the rule of law. They do not change with circumstances. Violating them is unethical—pure and simple.

On the other extreme are newly emerging values that are going to be tested—as with Napster, testing the limits of property rights in the Internet age. A new technological capability imposes a new demand, pushing the limits of the envelope.

So this core of invariants and periphery of things we experiment with as a society are separated by a zone, or ring, in between. The ring represents a middle ground where we have precedents and an emerging consensus, if not total agreement. Different views can persist. We are still working through the debate on foreign corrupt practices, but consensus is slowly emerging. We may have some rules, we may have some law, but we don't have the total consensus on this that we do on the invariants at the core, which have stood the test of time.

Core invariants to me represent ethical values. Emerging consensus is often represented by legal requirements. Pushing the envelope is about innovation, the use of new technologies for experimentation and creating new capabilities. As a society we need this portfolio. We cannot progress without experimenting at the margin.

In categories two and three—the emerging consensus and in pushing the envelope—you can expect misjudgments and misunderstandings as we find our way.

Where would you place Enron?

If it has violated core invariants, we should say so. We cannot and should not hide behind misjudgment of our core invariants in senior positions in public life. Neither should there be a question of interpretation of accounting rules.

As we evolve, our economy is going through a process of continuous change—deregulation, globalization, convergence of industries, Internet, biotech, and so on. We face multiple ethical dilemmas. It is an essential tension integral to the process.

However, moral lapses and the violation of core principles should not be confused with evolving uncertain or experimental business domains. We should hold fast and continuously reinforce core values that have served us so well and built a great republic, which never would—or should—stop experimenting at the margin.

We need innovation. We also need our anchors clean and clear. We must not forget our values—business, ultimately, is about it. If values are lost, everything is lost.

Exercises in Ethics

C. K. Prahalad describes business values as a dynamic combination of a center core of ethical standards that do not change over time, an outer ring made up of constantly changing new boundaries that evolve with the times and technology, and a middle ring of emerging consensus that develops with experience. (See diagram on next page.)

1. List two or three of these values for your organization in each of the rings shown in the diagram.

   a. Pushing the envelope (new boundaries, innovation)

   _____

   _____

   _____

   _____

   _____

   _____

   _____

   b. Emerging consensus (precedents, middle ground)

   _____

   _____

   _____

   _____

   _____

   _____

   _____

   c. Core ethics (the absolutes)

   _____

   _____

   _____

   _____

   _____

   _____

   _____

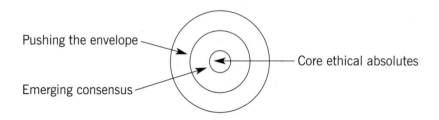

Pushing the envelope

Core ethical absolutes

Emerging consensus

2. Incorporate your explanation of these values and your rationale into your Teachable Point of View on business ethics.

_____

_____

_____

_____

_____

_____

_____

_____

_____

_____

_____

_____

_____

_____

_____

_____

_____

_____

_____

_____

_____

_____

_____

_____

6

We Need Great Leader-Teachers with Great Skills and High Ethics

Robert E. Knowling Jr.
Chief Executive Officer
New York Leadership Academy

Editors' Note: Want to build an ethical organization? Develop a clear Teachable Point of View, with business lessons and moral standards. Then, become a leader-teacher, and develop the leaders below you to be leader-teachers as well. Live your lessons. Model the process. Focus on it every day. Constantly share stories that are reinforcing and instructive. Lead and teach. What you'll end up with is a Virtuous Teaching Cycle with everyone teaching, everyone learning, and everyone becoming more aligned around shared values every day.

American business stands at a crossroads where it must get its ethical house in order. And yet, in 2002, these challenges are not new. The current environment is merely exposing the poor leadership that's been there all along.

Think Enron, WorldCom, Arthur Andersen, and the like.

When the economy was booming, too many inept leaders were able to ride the tide that lifted all boats. In our current environment, where market value has decreased some 40 percent to 90 percent in countless firms, the spotlight now shines on the business plan, the ability to execute, the ability to retain top talent, the ability to lead in difficult times, and—most of all—the ethics and credibility of the people in the company.

Going forward, successful companies and successful leaders will be those who understand that the greatest resource any business enterprise has is its people. Leaders who are entrusted with this human capital must develop all the individuals in their care into more valuable resources. And core to their development is instilling in these future leaders a sound ethical foundation to prepare them to deal with the decisions and dilemmas they will face down the road.

Delivered at the Hansen-Wessner Memorial Lecture, April 12, 2002, at the University of Michigan Business School, Ann Arbor, Michigan.

In business, the development of people can be a valuable competitive advantage. The role of a leader is, in some senses, like that of a parent. The leader must understand each employee's potential and then take the steps necessary to develop both their capabilities and their fundamental values. Leaders must also understand that they themselves are the primary role models. Inconsistent behavior or blurry ethical examples, such as waffling business norms, on their part will stand as a roadblock to developing others to be leaders.

■ Leading and Your Teachable Point of View

Difficult times require great leadership. People look to leaders when things are not going well. A leader must have a Teachable Point of View that describes where the company is headed and how it is going to get there, to give employees and shareholders the confidence they need.

In my tenure on the board at Heidrick & Struggles, I've seen the level of attention to leadership heighten as market conditions have eroded. Every CEO search keeps demonstrating the shortage of great leaders. The supply of jobs at the top is there, even in a down economy. The challenge is the scarcity of leader-teachers who will drive home the fundamentals of their business, as well as their commitment to conduct business in an ethical manner.

Effectiveness and efficiency are two elements of leadership that you hear a lot about. But they don't count for anything without strong ethics. I learned that on the basketball court. Although my basketball career has been over for some time, I can still recall the transformation that occurred between my junior and senior years in high school. I had played for a great coach in Indiana, Ben Bowles. He worked tirelessly with me year-round to make me the complete basketball player. I had set all sorts of scoring records my junior year and arguably was the finest basketball player in my area and one of the top players in the state. He had great plans for me—and it looked like we were going to make a run at the conference and state championships.

But then Coach Bowles left my school and was replaced by another Indiana high school legend, Dick Haslem. I did not bond with the new coach. I regarded him with a great deal of skepticism, and it was clear that he had a style that he wanted us to embrace that stressed ball movement—getting all five players in the mix—and strong defense.

A big preseason article came out on the team, and the new coach had this to say about me: "Bobby is perhaps the finest individual player that I have ever seen or coached, but he is going to have to make his teammates better and stay in a team game in order for us to be successful."

That, I now know, in one sentence reflected my new coach's ethics about high school sports—a fairness and equity where everyone plays and has a chance to excel, where everyone learns and teaches, where everyone gets better with the help of their teammates. But I didn't understand the coach's comment back then, and at seventeen, I didn't have the maturity to ask him about it.

We proceeded to go out and lose our first five games! We were highly ranked, I was highly decorated, and we started my senior year campaign 0–5!

Coach Haslem finally sat me down and taught me my first lesson on the ethics of leadership. I was scoring at will during those five losses, but there was no team. In fact, my teammates looked to me, deferred to me, and stood around watching me score. When the game was on the line, I didn't look for them and I surely didn't trust them to take a last shot.

I had to change—and I had to change quickly.

That season, I ended up scoring only eighteen points per game, way off my previous years, but we won the rest of our conference games and were the champs. I led the team in *assists* and two of my teammates received postseason awards for their play. It was the most gratifying athletic experience in my life—and I took away many valuable lessons.

■ Leaders Who Excel Must Also Teach

You can see this process played out in sports today from time to time. Larry Bird and Michael Jordan are two prime examples. Both were head and shoulders above everyone else in terms of their individual ability, but both brought out the best in their teammates to make their whole teams champions. They were able to lift the game of everyone around them because they invested in their teammates and made it their priority to help and teach others to reach their full potential.

The best kind of teaching takes place in what my friend Professor Noel Tichy calls Virtuous Teaching Cycles. These are cyclical processes in which the leaders are not only teachers but learners as well. As they share their ideas, knowledge, and values, they interact with their students. They engage them, and they listen to their responses. Then they revise their own ideas based on the input of their students and go out to teach some more.

It is a model that works. When I look at the successful championship runs of great CEOs such as GE's Jack Welch, Phil Condit at Boeing, John Chambers at Cisco, and several others, I see leaders who have made teaching, learning, and development a core ethic of their business. I see leaders making themselves vulnerable. I see them growing and developing just like everyone else in the organization. Herein lies the key to their success: They set an ethical standard in the company that it's OK not to have all the answers, OK that we don't have everything all figured out. It's even OK if we make mistakes sometimes. So, while these very direct, high-energy, and hard-driving CEOs command the complete attention of their organizations and have delivered stellar business results, they are real-life player-coaches employees can feel and touch.

It wasn't like that in my developmental years in the Bell System. That was a highly political environment that valued continuous learning on the technical side but largely ignored the possibility that any of its executives might need help with their leadership skills. Learning and growing on the job were signs of weakness, which led me to suppress any hint that I might be an incomplete product.

My orientation changed when I began to work with Noel Tichy. But it's important to note that I was a tough convert. I wasn't at all convinced about his methodology, so had it not been for the commitment of Bill Weiss (CEO of Ameritech) and later Dick Notebaert (successor to Weiss, currently CEO of Qwest) to change the Ameritech management system, I would probably not have come around. It was their embracing the process and their willingness to make themselves vulnerable that started me on a leadership learning journey that continues to this day.

Early on, I tried to thwart the Tichy program. He had been working very closely with the top 120 leaders of the company to help us reinvent the business. The process was long, painful, and time consuming, and we all still had our regular day jobs to do. The group of 120 had gotten together for four days with the senior leaders to assess progress and map out the next legs of the journey. One night, after a grueling day of debate and planning, I took the initiative in the bar to convince three of the four senior leaders to put a halt to a process we were about to go through. Tichy was going to have us numerically rank one another on how we were doing as team players, how much progress we were making at getting the transformational work done in the business, how well we assisted and helped others, and how much we were growing as leaders.

This process frightened me. I felt that the rankings would expose my weaknesses. I would be naked as a leader and, even worse, the exposure would come at the hands of my peers—the same peers I had competed against for years to get ahead in the game. I had been in plenty of close games before in my athletic career, and I'm the type of guy who wants the last shot, or the last at bat, or to be the guy with the ball in my hands when the game is on the line. This Tichy-devised process took the control completely away from me. I would clearly be exposed.

■ New Methods Can Make You Vulnerable

The next morning, after I did my insurrection and thought I had won, I remember Dick Notebaert coming to me and saying: "I think you're one of the most terrific people we've got in this business. You know how I feel about you. But there's a fundamental difference between you and me. I have navigated my career a lot like you have, all bent on my individual achievement, all about me, and the rest, but I've been exposed to some new things here and I've got a different perspective. The difference between you and me is that I'm willing to try this new stuff, I'm willing to make myself vulnerable, and you're not. But if somehow, Bob, you can trust this process and make yourself vulnerable and just be willing to try it, I think you might come out of this thing with a different perspective. My hope for you is that you don't bullshit the process and that you engage in it and do some analysis."

It hit me. If Dick was willing to try it, what did I have to lose? His participation and vulnerability really got me in the gut. It also marked an important inflection point in my career and in my journey. The forced rankings were the most emotional yet fulfilling developmental intervention in my entire career. The things that I feared would come out about my "Lone Ranger" style, indeed, did come out. The feedback was not filtered or sanitized, so it felt like a two-by-four across the head. On the other hand, I also got some wonderfully rewarding feedback on things I did exceptionally well that I had taken for granted. But, most important, this process allowed us senior executives to experience in real time the power of an emotionally shared experience. For us, it was the first encounter with open and candid feedback. It was so new to us that we even had a forum to talk about what had just happened to us. Confronting and getting through these emotions was an important watershed and a transformational experience for many of us.

It broke us out of the old bureaucratic silos. We were playing with real bullets or, to put it another way, doing total engine replacement while flying the aircraft. But this experience gave us the important transformational experience and building blocks that we needed to become leader-teachers.

The concept of a Virtuous Teaching Cycle is just that. Continuing your personal development and growth at the same time you are helping others reach their potential, with you as the role model teacher-coach. In any team endeavor, this is the ethical and right thing to do. Michael Jordan and Larry Bird did not just demand greatness of others, they led by example. It's common knowledge that Larry and Michael were fanatical about leadership and worked harder than anyone on their teams. They were first to practice and last to leave.

Similarly, Jack Welch didn't just make cameo appearances at GE's Crotonville leadership institute. He spent a significant amount of time there in the "Pit," teaching, learning, growing, developing others, and setting the example. I've had numerous sessions with former GE Appliances CEO Dick Stonesifer, whose stories about business reviews with Welch always hold something that he took away from the sessions in terms of his own development. Dick would turn around and model the same behavior or lesson with his direct reports, and they with theirs. I got a sense of how business lessons and business ethics dilemmas were shared across the GE system—replicated through this Virtuous Teaching Cycle, over and over.

■ Virtuous Cycle Built on Leaders Who Teach

For a Virtuous Teaching Cycle to work, the leaders must teach—and do it in an interactive way so that everyone gets smarter and better aligned. In my business, it starts with me: I require my leaders to teach. When I run a workshop with my leaders, I challenge them by telling them to embrace and engage in this process with me, because the requirement going forward is for them to emulate with their teams the experience we have been through. They, too, have to be the teachers. These are not workshops where consultants or staff are up front teaching; the leaders themselves are up front. If a sound ethical foundation is essential to become a leader, then the ability to teach and instill those sound ethical lessons in your people is essential for you to succeed as a leader.

It is scary, but rewarding.

I have been fortunate in my career to have had repeated opportunities to move on to bigger leadership positions. First, from an officer at Ameritech to a senior executive with wider responsibilities at U.S. West, then on to become CEO of Covad, and then to CEO at SimDesk Technologies. But this movement has had a downside—because I did not stay at any one place long enough to change the DNA of the organization, to ensure the perpetuation of the leadership cycle, the ethical lessons, and the business experiences and lessons.

Looking back, the most painful thing that I've gone through as a leader is leaving an organization and seeing the good work, the results of a lot of hard effort on my part and on the part of the brave and dedicated team members who worked with me, get erased because we didn't get the needed mindsets and values encoded deeply enough in the DNA of the organization. As someone with demanding ethical standards for both developing employees and maximizing the use of shareholder dollars, losing that potential makes me sad—even sick.

Developing a Teachable Point of View with a Virtuous Teaching Cycle to perpetuate it gives you the best chance at penetrating the organization's DNA quickly.

■ Transforming Business and Developing Leaders

At Ameritech, the leaders-developing-leaders model that Tichy helped us establish was incredibly powerful at both transforming the business and developing leaders. Note the number of current CEOs developed as a result of that process: Dick Notebaert at Qwest, Dick Brown at EDS, Gregg Brown at MicroMuse, Gary Drook at Affina, and John Edwards at CDW. However, during that time, Ameritech became so successful that SBC offered to buy it at a price shareholders couldn't refuse. SBC had a different management model and, as a result, the many great changes we had put in place at Ameritech slipped away because they hadn't had time to become sufficiently embedded in the organizational DNA.

When I became CEO of Covad, one of the first things I did was start a leaders-developing-leaders process. This allowed the business to get the right kind of framework so that we could grow in a disciplined way in the hypergrowth DSL world. But again, when I left, it hadn't taken root with the rank and file, and there wasn't a cadre of leaders who could then carry it on.

I now understand that the reason is that I didn't stay long enough. I don't care how good the group of immediate reports behind a CEO might be, long-term sustained leadership development will only happen when there is a CEO who is totally committed and focused on it. So if the CEO leaves before the process has reached throughout the organization and before the teaching and learning has become ingrained in the culture, it won't last. In the same way, a lack of CEO guidance on key ethical dilemmas facing the organization leaves the place "frozen" when it should be acting.

One key to Jack Welch's success in changing the DNA of GE was his longevity. Welch spent two decades building a new generation of leaders who not only carry on Virtuous Teaching Cycles at GE but build them in other companies when they leave. It's what Bob Nardelli is doing at Home Depot, Jim McNerney at 3M, and Tom Tiller at Polaris, to name but a few.

Another world-class leader-teacher I admire is Phil Condit, CEO of Boeing. I've had the good fortune to work side by side with him on the Hewlett-Packard board of directors. Condit typifies the impactful, important, ethical leader. His commitment to developing leaders is legendary—and it isn't just folklore. I have heard stories from Boeing employees about Condit and his leadership institute that send chills down my spine. And I have seen him in action. This man lives and breathes the importance of teaching.

Once when we were trying to set a quick date for a special board meeting, we ran into the traditional issues—director after director was going to be out of the country or on vacation for one date or another. The only time Phil posted an objection was when one of the potential dates conflicted with a commitment at the Boeing leadership institute. It struck me that one of the busiest executives in the world, who more than likely had the tightest calendar in the boardroom, was able to make other trade-offs on his time to make the board meetings. But when it came to his commitment to leadership development, this was sacred. I'm not sure that an invitation from the president of the United States could get Condit to miss a commitment to his leadership institute. But, I have no doubt that when Condit retires, his legacy of leadership development, like Welch's, will survive in the company.

That's what leaders will have to do to win in the twenty-first century—as Phil Condit and Jack Welch did—build organizations with strong ethics and knowledge creation embedded in their DNA, where people teach and learn interactively and instinctively.

Tichy's Virtuous Teaching Cycle cracks the code on how to institutionalize the process and become a great leader. Start with a Teachable Point of View rich in business experiences, with ethical lessons that model, with visions of where you are taking the organization. Teach it. Discuss. Learn. Refine. Proliferate the message. Live the message. And keep it up—for years. The resulting Virtuous Teaching Cycle is the best way to spread key business lessons and to instill ethical standards for your people to follow. That's what leadership is all about.

Exercises in Ethics

What's your life story? You'll find that your own life experiences contribute to who you are as a leader, as they did for Bob Knowling, and to your Teachable Point of View on ethics.

1. The best way we know to help develop your own story is to draw your Personal Journey Line, reflecting emotional highs and lows throughout your life. Do this by going left-to-right on a chart like the one shown on the following page, placing dots at the key influence points throughout your life, with a word or two describing the event. Then draw a line connecting the dots.

HIGH

LOW _____

TIME

2. How did issues on the following list and other influences specific to your own life provide key developmental moments and contribute to shaping who you are as a leader?

- Where you were born and raised
- Parents
- Family values
- Siblings
- Education
- Socioeconomics
- Examples of success or failure
- Discrimination
- Life challenges
- Work career experiences
- Tough decisions and choices
- Developing other leaders
- Career paths
- Business integrity
- Business sense and judgment

- Personal relationships
- Marriage
- Children
- Health
- Sports/Coach
- Teamwork
- Changing perspectives
- Beyond-comfort challenges
- Rapid advancement
- Having boss that limits you
- Leadership
- Learning
- Teaching
- Doing the "right thing"
- Creating your Teachable Point of View

_____

_____

_____

3. One important way to strengthen your Teachable Point of View on business ethics is to include a few examples from your personal experiences. These bring credibility and the authority of experience to your message, especially when personalizing the experiences makes you a little vulnerable in the process. Develop one or two such personal references that contributed to your formative experiences and learning on ethics and integrity in business and incorporate them into your Teachable Point of View on business ethics.

_____

_____

_____

_____

_____

_____

_____

_____

4. What processes exist within your organization where elements of Virtuous Teaching Cycles exist—where leaders act as both teachers and learners?

_____

_____

_____

_____

_____

5. If these processes do not fulfill the requirements for complete Virtuous Teaching Cycles, what elements can be added to improve them?

Leaders Teaching	*Leaders Learning*
▪ _____	▪ _____
▪ _____	▪ _____
▪ _____	▪ _____
▪ _____	▪ _____

7

Ethics "Honor One's Self" in Your Business Behavior

Robert Dolan
Dean and Professor
University of Michigan Business School

n *Ethical Ambition,* Derrick Bell defines "ethical living" as "an ongoing commitment, as we meet life's day-to-day challenges and opportunities, to assume risk in honor of self and all others."

This definition provides us the thought-provoking idea that to be ethical is to assume risk. In other words, it is an act of courage. And the purpose of being ethical is to honor one's self.

What does it mean to be courageous in business decision making? Should one "honor one's self" through business decision making? And if so, how?

Those are some of the key questions that the material in this book probe and illuminate. Business is a noble profession. At its heart, it is, as Peter Drucker said long ago, about creating and keeping a customer. One creates and keeps a customer by combining ideas, resources, and processes in a way that delivers true value to customers—at a cost below that value. Business is thus an instrument of social welfare.

It is, as recent events attest, an instrument that sometimes breaks. Unethical behavior by executives can destroy the nobility of business pursuits. Many have, of course, written on the issue of business ethics. Much of this writing is in the form of exhortations to do well with the assurance that "ethics is good business." If this were uniformly the case—that by the usual calculus used to measure business performance and evaluate executives, it was good to be ethical—being ethical would hardly be an act of courage.

Consider this scenario. On the eve of disclosure of its quarterly sales figures, a young, on-the-rise publicly traded company, one that has met "street expectations" every quarter so far, realizes that it will fall 5 percent short of the $20 million sales figures it told Wall Street to expect. The reception this announcement will receive is not difficult to predict—the stock price will be punished severely. Employee morale will suffer as options go "under water." The firm's momentum will stall and be difficult to regain.

Yet a number of big sales are in the works and on the very edge of closing. Certainly, a million dollars of sales will close in the next couple of weeks—purchase authorizations are just making their way through the buying organizations. Wouldn't "good business" dictate a little latitude in counting the sales as done—so the company's hard-won reputation as an up-and-comer could be maintained, as well as employee morale? Should it matter that much if a sale comes through in early April rather than late March?

Maybe it shouldn't. Maybe the way stocks are evaluated is flawed—but that's a discussion for another day. It did matter a lot. To do the right thing, to be ethical was, in short, by the scorecard of many, very costly.

This book presents not hypothetical stories but real senior executives and University of Michigan Business School faculty who have observed lots of others, dealing with the fact that maintaining one's integrity can come at an enormous price by some accountings. How did they think about this? Where did they find the courage to bear the short-term consequences and "honor one's self" and others by doing the right thing?

This is the kind of question we need to address rather than add more feeling to exhortations to do well. We hope this volume helps people to develop the right measures of success—measures in the spirit of that proposed by Peter Gomes in *The Good Life*, especially in his chapter, "Success: How Do I Know When I Have Made It?" It characterizes success as "less in achieving what one set out to do but more in doing something that is worth doing."

Exercises in Ethics

Living ethically in business takes courage and assumes risk.

1. Write an example of a risk you have taken in business because of your ethical standards.

_____

_____

_____

_____

_____

_____

_____

_____

_____

2. Write an example of an occasion where you showed courage in the
   face of an ethical challenge.

_____

_____

_____

_____

_____

_____

_____

_____

3. Incorporate these examples into your Teachable Point of View on
   business ethics to provide examples and context to your employees
   and other constituents.

_____

_____

_____

_____

_____

_____

_____

_____

_____

PART 2

The Aftermath

The months that followed the seemingly daily admissions and confessions by company after company made it clear that what happened at Enron was not an isolated incident. The basic ethics and integrity of American business were being challenged, questioned, doubted, and mistrusted. What would business do to respond?

GE Chairman Jeffrey Immelt begins by saying it's not enough anymore for business to merely obey the law and consider that a statement of ethics and integrity. Immelt characterizes obeying the law as the "low bar," something that businesses must dramatically exceed to make a real mark. Professor Anjan Thakor likens that extra step to keeping not just the explicit commitments a business makes to constituents but also the implicit contracts that are conveyed by the company's image and reputation. Both Immelt and Thakor agree those extra efforts allow businesses to build reputational premiums, which allow them to receive price premiums from their customers.

Steelcase Chairman James Hackett underscores how doing the ethical thing in business isn't always easy. He recounts his decision, against a backdrop of other negative business events, to recall a wall-panel product because it did not meet the highest in flammability standards—and the pride that decision caused weeks later, during a day of national disaster. Professor Robert Quinn characterizes such tough decisions as being made when we as human beings take an unnatural approach to decision making, something that distinguishes real leaders.

Trilogy founder Joe Liemandt contrasts how the times have changed basic business methods, requiring a transition from the "anything goes" spirit of the dot-com era to one of a higher responsibility to partner with customers and ensure that they get what they wanted from your product as a sign of business integrity. Professor Kim Cameron likens that important change and evolution to something that should occur when you can stay focused and not lose your bearings despite the dynamic turbulence going on around you and your business.

Professor Tim Fort underscores the importance of people's values-related experiences and the resulting teaching they do to build organizations committed to high ethical standards in business.

8

Values

The Best Tools to Lead a Large Global Organization

Jeffrey Immelt
Chairman and Chief Executive Officer
General Electric Company

Editors' Note: Values—of leaders and of their organizations—are critical to leading global organizations to new heights. Jeff Immelt leads by values. He drives home the point every day in myriad ways, from emphasizing the importance of giving back to society to providing equal opportunities for success to all employees—whether in Los Angeles or Lagos. Immelt's values are the driving principle behind his far-sighted view on honesty and business ethics. He insists that simply obeying the law is just too little and that future leaders—in his company and beyond—must aim higher, for the ultimate benefit of the world they will inherit.

The most important thing I learned in two years of business school is that there are twenty-four hours in a day—and you can use all of them when you must.

It's served me well over the years. Sleep while you can.

I'd like to frame the importance of giving back—what I think of as integrity—in the framework that I see for total leadership, so you can think of it from top to bottom, because it's important to see how the pieces fit together.

I see leadership on four levels.

■ Constantly Refocus for the Future

First, leading a big company like GE really does start with strategy. It starts with knowing what to do, what you're good at, what you're not good at, and constantly refocusing the company for the future.

It means you always have to be very vigilant about seeing the world for what it is, making the tough resource allocation choices, taking your organization always into the future.

In GE, it starts with the businesses we're in. It's not that hard, intellectually. It really isn't. You just have to be open and always be watching. And you have to always be focused on getting what you're really good at aligned with the businesses you're in—so you can constantly create value.

In GE today, about 70 percent of the company is exactly where I want us to be for the twenty-first century. And about 30 percent isn't. So we constantly have to make these tough resource allocation calls about what we want to do and what we don't want to do. That's a part of what a leader does.

■ Learning New Things All the Time

The second thing is you must expand the horizon for what your company really can be. You have to be learning all the time. You really have to build a learning organization and drive initiatives through the organization.

Jack Welch had initiatives like Six Sigma in the past.

We've got four initiatives that we're driving across the company today.

- Technology: We want to make GE a high-tech leader for the twenty-first century.
- Markets: We want to make GE more global, take it to places like China, and to Europe in a big way, because we see these as markets of the future.
- Digitization: We want to use resources to change the shape of the company—smaller backrooms, larger front rooms.
- Customers: We're a very customer-focused company—and we want to always be on the same side as the customer. So we really want to drive services and continue to evolve our strategy, driving service with our customers.

It's not that important what these initiatives are today. What is important is to always be picking things up that will expand the boundaries of your organization. And always picking what's going to be next.

When you pick those things, you have a constituency of one. Change in any big organization, in the beginning, has a constituency of one. But, as a leader, you have to have the passion and the drive to make sure it happens.

■ Aligning Head, Heart, and Wallet

The third thing I think a lot about, with respect to leadership, is alignment. I have three hundred thousand people who work for me at General Electric. How do you capture them?

What you must have at any point is complete alignment between the head, the heart, and the wallet. Head, heart, wallet. You have to be teaching people all the time. They have to be learning new tricks, new tools, new processes that can constantly invigorate them, constantly leave them on the edge of their seat for new directions, being smarter and knowing what to do.

And you have to measure them. Those measurements have to be backed with rewards—financial rewards—with complete alignment between thinking and doing and compensation.

But that's not enough today. Because people have to believe in something—they have to have heart. They have to have a mission that they think is unbeatable. And they have to feel like they're going to play with a team that will help them get there.

And people today—in every company, in every part of the world, every place I go—know part of that mission can't just be business, part of it can't just be beating competition or increasing shareholder value. They are all necessary—no less intensely so than they've been in the past. But that's not enough anymore. People want to be part of companies that are doing great things. They want to be part of companies that are taking small ideas into big places. And they want to be a part of something that can make a difference.

Nobody ever wants to go to work for a big company. Nobody ever dreams, when they're young, about going to work for GE someday. You want to be part of a place where you can build your dreams.

I never once talk about GE as being a big company. I think about GE as a company that has the resources, people, and capability that allows people to build their dreams.

For most people, building their dreams is about taking a business from zero to $10 billion in a decade. We can do that.

A lot of people who work for us want to make scanners that can save people, see a day when GE can be building factories in Africa or inner-city Detroit or other places around the world. They want to be part of a company that makes a difference in the world.

I worry a lot about the head. I worry a lot about the wallet, because those things are important. But I worry as much today about the heart, making sure that this is a company where people want to work, where they want to give something back, and where they know they can make a difference all the time.

It starts with strategy. Then building broader horizons. Then alignment—head, heart, wallet.

■ Bad Values Can Kill You

And the last thing a company must stand for is values.

We've witnessed, over the last six to nine months in this country, what I would say is the equivalent of a corporate freak show. It's been a time when everything's been reversed, when all our excesses have been exposed.

And I'm here to tell you, it's going to change. The changes will be for the better. Some of it is about pure criminality, but a lot of it's just about bad values.

The thing that always worries me, when I run GE, is that bad things can happen to our company when the wrong ten people get together at the wrong time. You can never do enough to make sure that you protect a company of three hundred thousand people. But when the wrong ten people are in the boardroom, real damage can happen.

The way you deal with that is by driving values all the time. We spend a billion dollars a year in training, to make sure that we embed in our people values and openness. We grade all our top leaders not just on performance but on values. We pay people in the same currency—dollars or GE stock. So everybody is aligned completely in terms of what they do. And the last thing, we don't put up with anybody who gets close to the values line. GE is a company where one strike and you're out.

I was with an investor earlier and he asked if GE has a policy against executives taking IPO stock from investment bankers we do business with. The thought of somebody taking stock in an IPO—the thought of having a separate financial entity that a CFO can run—those are things that great companies can't have. Values *are* the critical difference.

And when you look at some of the things that have happened in corporate America today, it's not driven by stock options. It's not driven by people driving too hard. It's driven by bad cultures and bad values.

Make sure that you stand up every day for performance with integrity.

■ **CEO: Moral Leader of the Company**

The CEO today has to be the moral leader of the company—the way you talk about your company externally and the way you run it internally.

There must be crystal clear transparency about companies today. More will be known, more will be shown, and you can't even think about running the company any differently than you're willing to talk about externally. That's extremely important. And every great company must have it.

You must have external checks and balances, outsiders that help govern—a board of directors. They'll be nearly 100 percent outsiders, with no links. And I think that's great, because the more smart people we have looking at our company, the better I think we can do.

Lastly, you must have pay plans and compensation from the CEO on down that are totally aligned with investors. So the changes we're making are for every leader in GE to hold a bunch of GE stock and to make sure that they never can cash a stock option less than one year after they receive it—a one-year holding period. So we're always aligned with investor interest. I want GE not only to perform—performance is a given—but I want us to be a company that everybody can look up to and respect, that every employee inside the company is always proud of.

One of the most important things you can do for yourself is define success.

I'm here mainly because I'm lucky. My father worked in GE's aircraft engine factory in Cincinnati. My parents were tremendous and always said, "You can do it. Whatever you put your mind to do, you can do it. We'll pay for an education—and you can take an education and go where you can go in your life."

My dream was to be the best I could be.

In my lifetime, I've had a chance to make a difference.

I have even more passion each day. You know, I get a lot of crappy feedback every day—a stock price that drops, or an irate employee, stuff like that. It doesn't hurt me. It makes me want to show them even more.

■ Managing Time Is Critical

So every day I live, I get more passionate. I get more mad at myself, I can't go faster. Now, I've also got a family that I love. Probably the most critical thing I manage in my world is time. I've got a job with an infinite amount of work. I could work 102 hours a day, if I wanted to. So you make choices. I've got a wife, I've got a great daughter, things I like to do with them—and so I regulate myself by making choices about time, making sure I get enough to be a balanced person and do all the other things I like in the world.

But if you like business and you like people, I've got the best job in the world.

You may want to be CEO of a company someday, but you go to work for a consulting firm. Why? That's not following the path of your dream. If you want to be a good consultant, be a good consultant. Go on that path. But if you want to be a CEO, go to work for a company.

If you want to do a start-up, do a start-up. But really live with a real focus on what you want to do, your plan to get there, the path you want to go along, and learn that the most valuable part of any education is the capacity for learning.

You may define success from a standpoint of how far you want to go in a company. You may want a job like this one, that's great. You may define it by what you want to build, by personal freedom, by financial freedom, by being able to have global assignments, that's great. You may define it based on having a successful business and having a great personal life, I think those things are all fabulous. But I hope the way you define it is on how much you can give—not what you can take.

I'm the CEO of GE. But when I go home, the way I define what I've had the privilege of being able to do here is have the unique opportunity to build my dreams, to make a difference with people who are my friends. That's success. I have the ability to give back. We have the ability to do many different things.

■ The Decade of the Givers

I can spot in an instant, within our company, the givers and the takers. And, I think the givers are the ones who will succeed in the next decade. The givers are the ones who will succeed in your lifetime. People who do great work, who give back to the workplace, who make a difference in their communities.

One of the things you'll confront in your lifetime is the uprising of the disenfranchised in the world—the sense that fatcat bosses have ruined the world. They have people being led off in handcuffs to corroborate that. The disenfranchised stand up now and say corporations are bad, globalization's bad, things like that.

I think globalization is tremendously important, in terms of the future, not just from an economic standpoint but from a social standpoint. Think about it in its totality.

It starts with going where the customers are. Now there are a lot of customers in China. You must go there and find ways to sell your products, jet engines, CT scanners, because that's what your business needs. But if you just take that step, it's not enough.

The second thing you must be committed to do is improve intellectual and human capital everywhere in the world. If you're in China, you can't just sell CT scanners. You must be committed to make CT scanners in China, to invest in engineering, capability, training. You have to invest in all those things. When we build factories around the world, they have the same environmental standards and quality standards as a factory would have in the U.S.

Today that's not enough, either. The third thing you must do is make a commitment to the people. And within GE, basically the philosophy I try to uphold everywhere is that no matter where you join our company and walk in the door—whether it's India or China or Saudi Arabia or France—if you have the aspiration and ability, you should be able to have the same personal dream that somebody has if they join in Detroit, Connecticut, or anyplace else. So all our people get treated the same way. They all get training, the same education, and we try to make sure they all get the same opportunities.

I think if you do those three things, you don't look like a colonialist. You look like an investor. You look like a long-term player, somebody who cares.

It's tough to go everywhere in the world. You have to pick your spots. I believe in India. I believe in China. I believe in Russia. I believe in Eastern Europe. It's tougher for me to invest—take our investors' money—to places where I don't think we have a chance, legally, to get our money back because the rule of law cannot be upheld, or things like that.

■ Global Leaders for Global Businesses

I make four trips to Europe and three trips to Asia each year, each at least a week long. I spend time visiting with employees, customers, government officials, doing business reviews. So I know the people and the regions—and I've done business in almost all parts of the world, so I have a pretty good instinctive feel for it.

We don't have a bunch of Americans running these businesses around the world. In Korea most of our business leaders are Korean. In Japan most of our business leaders are Japanese. In Europe most of our leaders are European. So we have Europeans and Asians here running businesses, investing in developing people over long periods of time.

They grew up in their native culture, know the GE culture, and put the two together. It's very important to know local customs. You won't be successful unless you understand the difference between Korea, Japan, and China, for instance, and the way customers interact.

But we also never change our values. In other words, I could get more engine business in certain places around the world if I used facilitating payments and government agents. I don't do that. I don't want to do that. That's a GE custom—and I don't care what the local custom is. So sometimes it's important to have local understanding, sometimes it's important not to have local understanding—if it doesn't fit your own legal structure or your own set of values.

■ Marrying Your Values, Local Customs

All of globalization is this marriage between understanding local customs and never running away from who you are and what you stand for on a global basis. Our values are global. Our rules and our culture are global. And I hope it gets better every day because we have more employees in China, India, Korea, or Europe.

But it's always this blending of the two.

There are parts of the world where the legal and social structures aren't equipped for me to put money there yet. And in those places, what we have to do is find ways to take CT scanners, medical equipment, and things that we can do that are good—and make sure they get to some of those people to help them.

It takes a sense of globalization in its totality with a corporate spirit to give more than you take. And if you do those things, I think the world opens up.

But it's a fight you need to be willing to fight, because there's a whole community that believes that Americans taking business to China is evil, that people in Mexico doing work that could be done here is bad. There are people in Europe who say a product that's made here shouldn't be shipped there.

We'll have to make this world an open place. That's not a job, that's an imperative—an economic and moral imperative. And you fight it by calling on customers, building capability, and investing in people.

I started my career in selling at GE. I never really planned to do that. I was in our plastics business, was graduating from business school and had a product management assignment at headquarters. I said if you really want to learn a business, you should learn it from the ground floor someplace. Pick manufacturing, or pick sales, or something like that.

So I asked for an assignment in sales and became a sales manager for our plastics business in Dallas. I fell in love with it. I love the immediacy. I love the touch of it. And what it taught me, at a very early point in my career, is how to look at our businesses from the outside in, how to look at a strategy from the standpoint of the people who actually bought what you were selling.

■ Of Customers and Headquarters

Why did most dot-com companies fail?

It wasn't because of technology. It was because they didn't have any customers.

You look at any business and in the beginning, there was an order.

It helped me.

I hate headquarters. I spent the first ten years of my career hating headquarters. I hate it today. I'm a cynic about headquarters. I'm into what's real. I like touching customers. I just finished two days, four cities, meeting 250 customers at a time, hearing about what's going on, sharing ideas, things like that.

It gave me a sense of how to look at companies. And it also drilled in me two things that good salespeople have: great listening skills and a sense of urgency.

I've built my career in other functions, other jobs, to the job I have today. But I've never gone to a meeting where I didn't ask more questions than I answered—and I never go to sleep at night until everything that's important is done. And those are two skills I learned out in the field that have served me well every step of the way.

And I talk a lot about pushing boundaries all the time. It's part of being a learning organization. I spend a lot of time on the road. I spend a lot of time with other CEOs, a lot of time with customers. And I'm always looking for what that next idea can be, what the next way to get better is. I never assume that we're the best at anything, because we're probably not. I'm always looking for those one, or two, or three ideas—at any given point in time—and finding ways to take those back and change the way the company's shaped, change how fast you can do something.

An example right now—one of the real dividends of the Internet and the digital age—is that information technology changes the way you can run a company. I'm convinced that we can take jobs—front room jobs, backroom jobs, customer-touching jobs, growth-oriented jobs, high-value jobs, and jobs that we've just crowded into administrative centers where people really aren't that happy—and use technology to dramatically change the way our company looks.

That's what I mean by changing the boundaries, by finding ideas, by learning.

You can't have too many initiatives, only a select few. But you can really change the notion of expanding the capacity, expanding the boundaries. And that's how you grow an organization.

■ What Determines Who You Are?

You know, particularly in a big company like GE, a performance company, your own self-confidence and self-worth help dictate and frame who you are.

When I look at moral leadership—I worked for Jack Welch the last five or six years and Jack was a demanding boss—but I decided a long time ago, that Jack Welch never could determine whether I was good or bad. Only I could determine that.

He could ask me to leave. He could ask me to stay. He could ask me to do a bunch of different stuff.

But leadership and growth in anything is an intensive journey in understanding yourself.

I decided early on that my job wasn't to follow Jack. My job was to lead GE in a new century, with a new team, with a group of people that basically didn't think it was just about him. We thought it was about all of us. We think this great company's about all of us. It's not fundamentally about a star system. It's a company that's about a system, a process, a culture—from Thomas Edison to Jack Welch, the tapestry of time.

Inside the company, it's been a very natural process. I never once had to worry for one second about my team. I've gotten 100 percent of their support. It's been a natural transition.

Now, I had a great predecessor. Jack has been fabulous. He's done nothing but help build my confidence. He never calls me. But if I call him—and sometimes I might call him two or three times a week—he's there to talk, to listen, to bounce ideas off.

So if you have a great predecessor, if you have your own self-confidence in the things you want to do, and you have a tremendous team that's totally aligned, the transition can be smooth and natural.

Now I've had one advantage—and that is that the last year has been truly bizarre in every way. From 9/11, that great tragedy, to all the things that happened, in some ways, it's been a silver lining for me. It's a new day and new leadership's required.

We'll need new skills in our leaders. You'll need to ask: How can I get better? Where can I improve? What's my self-worth? What do I respect? What do I want?

■ Forging Your Moral Leadership

A lot about moral leadership gets forged by your learning, your comfort with yourself, your deeply rooted values.

You get into all these debatable, moralistic dilemmas about whether you lay people off, or ever do this or do that. My first thought is that values aren't necessarily about being nice. Values are about being consistent, about being direct, making choices. Values are about having firmly rooted strengths in places where you never blink.

One big moral dilemma I had, within GE, was when I was running our plastics business, in the mid-1990s and we had massive inflation. Plants blew up and a whole series of things went on. We had a couple hundred million dollars of inflation and the only way to recoup the inflation was to raise the selling price, immediately, on our products. And we had a bunch of fixed-price contracts.

Some managers felt that in such a crisis we should raise prices. But, I said no. We waited six months.

In that time, I would tell customers, "You can pay me now or you can pay me later, but you are going to pay me." But I did it within the construct of the contracts. And when those contracts were up, we got our price increase. I took a lot of hits. I missed my numbers for a year—I was firmly in Jack's doghouse.

But those are dips that you take in your career. I'm not here because I have a perfect career or because I'm perfect. I'm here because I make the same mistake only once. I learn pretty quickly. That's what you should do in your career. Learn.

Where does my attention go?

■ Employees First and Foremost

At this time of great disruption, I worry about our employees first and foremost. Our employees own about 10 percent of the company. They are what make us a great company. Every other week I do an e-mail, I do a webcast quarterly to more than 250,000 employees. I respond to all employee e-mail myself. I do a dinner a week. I teach at Crotonville once a month. And I spend an incredible amount of time so that our employees know that whatever they read about other companies—you know World-Com, Tyco, Enron, a whole series of other companies—that it has nothing to do with GE.

I'm not saying we're a perfect company. We've got problem businesses. We've got businesses that aren't doing as well as they should. We have employees we must fire every day for disciplinary reasons, stuff like that. But this is a 124-year-old company. We stand for something. It's a company where every senior leader has as their No. 1 aspiration that we leave the place better than when we came here. We reemphasize that with employees each and every day.

So you always have to make sure your employees know what you stand for, who you are, how you get paid, and that you're in it for them and with them; you know, in it together.

This stuff's going to pass. But the notion that the only thing a CEO has to do is be honest sets the threshold way too low.

Honesty should be assumed—and it's about performance. That's what our people want and that's what they expect.

Exercises in Ethics

Jeff Immelt contends that merely being honest sets too low a threshold for business ethics and integrity. He believes that total transparency—to insiders and outsiders—will be required for a company to be truly great in the future.

1. Think about such transparency and your own organization—and how complete that transparency may be. What activities, if any, could hurt your organization's public image if they were to be revealed to the external public?

_____

_____

_____

_____

_____

_____

_____

2. How could the exposure of this information harm your organization's reputation?

_____

_____

_____

3. How could the problems be alleviated so that your organization could move toward total transparency?

_____

_____

_____

4. Formulate how solving that challenge could enhance your organization's credibility and strengthen your Teachable Point of View on business ethics, providing an instructive example of your stand on business ethics.

_____

_____

_____

_____

_____

_____

9

Competence Without Credibility Won't Win in the Long Run

Anjan Thakor
Professor of Banking and Finance
University of Michigan Business School

Editors' Note: The value of ethical conduct in business has been a sub-ject of longtime debate among economists. But the value is highlighted when viewed in terms of our "implicit contracts" with customers and constituents. Those assurances reflect our standards and fundamental beliefs in doing the right thing. This is what allows a company to build credibility and respect, which ultimately also allows it to charge price premiums for products or services. Those excess funds provide impor-tant fuel in a cycle that then goes on to financially enable doing more "right things." Strong ethics power a dynamic capital market system envied throughout the world.

E thics has often been considered a "soft" topic in business, but as the Enron–Arthur Andersen episodes underscore, having ethics is a matter of critical importance. A good code of ethics among corporate executives is central to the way our capital markets work. Without a good code of ethics, em-ployees and investors lose confidence and the capital markets can't function.

Most people understand that strong markets are built on functioning legal systems. The origins of legal systems relate to contract enforcement. And contract enforcement determines how active a capital market can be—such things as how many IPOs are issued and how many companies exist per ten thou-sand people, key indicators of such financial development.

An exciting new area of research has found that how we enforce contracts and the rights of creditors matters in the de-velopment of sophisticated financial markets. You can't just go into an emerging country and say, "Well, if you just have good financial markets, you'll be like the U.S." They need the right legal system and enforcement of contracts for a capital market to develop and then to operate beneficially.

■ Ethics Represent "Implicit Contracts"

Ethics can be thought of in business as the "implicit contracts" that represent who you are and what you stand for. These are the things your constituents expect to rely on, even if they aren't explicitly stated in a written contract. Implicit contracts reflect your ethical core. The dividing line between law and ethics is a constantly moving one. What is legal but unethical today may well become illegal tomorrow.

Economists see being ethical as nothing more than honoring implicit contracts with investors, creditors, employees, senior executives, and other constituents. And it makes good business sense—not necessarily in the short term but always in the long run—to honor these implicit contracts.

In a purely business sense, being ethical means going beyond the fine print of a contract. It means doing what's right for the customer just because it is in keeping with the spirit of the contract, if not the letter.

Somebody doesn't pay you $20 million, for instance, to get a product that meets the specifications but doesn't do the work they bought it to do. And when you take on the responsibility for making it work so that the customer does get the benefit, you develop a reputation—which is a very real economic concept.

Brand equity, credibility, and reputation are all just different names for something that translates into dollars and cents. That's because customers are willing to pay more for products and services that they trust. You buy a McDonald's burger not because it's the best food in the world but because you know what you're getting. There's credibility. It has a point along the value spectrum that people understand—a reputation for consistency the world over.

Reputation is a very valuable economic good. When people risk theirs by becoming unethical, it is almost always because they saw some kind of short-term financial gain to be made in doing the unethical thing. Think about it as taking your stock of "reputational capital" and liquefying it—selling it. It's a little like selling your left kidney—you get money, but lose a piece of yourself in the process.

And reputation is a lot easier to lose than it is to build. That's the thing that people too often forget.

If you're GE or any company that's doing well financially and also has a lot of reputational capital, you have a lot to lose by being unethical. After all, when you do something unethical, it's not likely that somebody will say, "Well, we'll take away 5 percent of your reputational capital for that little sin."

You can lose it all! Arthur Andersen is a great example. There was one major instance of wrongdoing, at Enron. But people didn't say, "We'll just pay Andersen 5 percent less because they don't have as much brand equity as they did before Enron." No. The whole thing was lost. And the bigger the reputation you have, the more you have to lose when you jeopardize it.

■ **Ethical Companies Won't Risk "Brand Equity"**

Companies that have been ethical, that have built up a reputation, have a greater incentive in economic terms to hang onto their brand equity—and not to do anything that might even risk it.

If you're a nobody faced with an ethical dilemma, you might feel that you have nothing to lose by going over the line. Perhaps that contributed to some of the recent wrongdoing by U.S. companies. But customers, too, know the new guys may be willing to make big risky bets, and that may be why big customers often prefer to deal with established businesses.

Interestingly, if you have a lot of brand equity, you're likely to be doing well financially because you're able to charge a premium. And with that financial strength, you are better able to cope ethically with dilemmas. You have the financial wherewithal to say, "You know what? We'll fix this at our expense, even though it's not in the contract." If you're financially strapped, then that may be more than you feel you can afford.

But this doesn't mean that all start-ups are unethical or that they can't compete with older companies. Thanks to healthy capital markets, a new business built on the right ideas and values can go public to raise capital. This is part of the natural process of evolution for an organization and the reason capital markets exist. It's actually very healthy.

A very important difference exists between the extent of entrepreneurial funding in the U.S. relative to, say Europe, for instance. It has always been a lot easier for a high-tech, high-risk venture to find venture capital funding—long before going public—in the U.S. than in Europe.

Why?

One hypothesis that makes a lot of sense is that venture capitalists need exit options. And a new firm's going public is really more for the investor or person taking the initial financial risk than for the company's founders. If I'm an entrepreneur, I can't get bank funding because I don't have any assets to offer as collateral. I need money to grow my business, but it's very difficult to get venture funding if the venture capitalist cannot see a clear exit option at the end of four or five years. And that exit option most often comes in the firm's going public. Before they get in, investors want to know that they can liquefy their claims and get out of an investment.

In Europe, capital markets are not as receptive to smaller high-tech, risky start-ups, so it's not that easy for small companies to get going. Venture investment companies may see themselves as stuck in a private equity deal for ten or fifteen years, so they avoid going into it in the first place.

■ Virtues of the U.S. Capital Market

From the standpoint of financing start-up ventures, which is what gets innovation and entrepreneurship going, the U.S. capital market system is tremendous. And one fear is that in the wake of Enron and Andersen and all the other troubles, we will lose sight of its virtues and throw out the baby with the bathwater. We must not forget that it is still the best financial market in the world. Sometimes we have a propensity to compare ourselves with Utopia.

In the 1990s, when it came to IPOs, a lot of people were starting up stupid things that had no sound business model. A lot of money chased ideas and a lot of things got started that never should have been funded. And some of their promoters just wanted to cash out of the IPOs, with no desire to really build or run a business.

Some of the worst ethical abuses occurred in the late 1990s and early 2000s in connection with IPOs, with people selling out their personal stock stakes when they knew that the company wasn't doing well. Some even were selling while they talked up the stock to others. And for some the profits were enormously high—though rooted in questionable ethics.

But every once in a while, these things have to happen. They're actually good. They may seem very bad in the short run, but in the long run, they make us realize where the loopholes in our system are and what needs to be fixed.

When everything was going great in the 1990s, it wasn't as if people were oblivious to the potential pitfalls. It's just that nobody had the time or the interest to do anything about them. Everybody was too busy making money.

But whether they're students just starting their careers or executives toward the end of theirs, I've never met anybody who was sorry for having done the right thing and for being ethical. Even if they don't make huge sums of money, they have a tremendous personal satisfaction and pride when they look in the mirror.

At the end of the day, all our MBAs will make more than enough money to get by. So it's not as if they'll need to be unethical to survive.

More important, it comes down to feeling good about yourself and what you're doing with your life, and that—in the end—may be the most important reason to behave ethically.

And, for executives, there is also the matter of corporate success. In the long run, it is very difficult for a company to be successful if the CEO and senior management don't have credibility with Wall Street, or their employees, or with investors. Without that credibility, nobody will trust their financial statements or their projections, or believe them when they say, "This is my new strategy."

So in business you can't really function without credibility. And credibility requires at the very least that you be ethical. It's not sufficient to be ethical, of course; you also must be very good at what you do in terms of competence. But competence without credibility won't win in the long run.

Exercises in Ethics

Anjan Thakor underscores the importance of a company's going beyond its explicitly stated contractual commitments to certain "implicit contracts," which represent the organization's core values and ethics.

1. What are the "implicit contracts" that your company has with customers, employees, shareholders, the community, and other constituencies?

   a. Customers:

   _____

   _____

   _____

☐

b. Employees:

_____

_____

_____

c. Shareholders:

_____

_____

_____

d. Community:

_____

_____

_____

e. Other:

_____

_____

_____

2. How does maintaining these "implicit contracts" bring added value to your business—through enhanced reputation, brand equity, and so on—and provide your company added credibility with those constituencies?

a. Customers:

_____

_____

_____

b. Employees:

_____

_____

_____

c. Shareholders:

_____

_____

_____

d. Community:

_____

_____

_____

e. Other:

_____

_____

_____

3. How can these value explanations contribute to and be incorporated to add value to your Teachable Point of View on business ethics?

_____

_____

_____

_____

_____

_____

_____

_____

_____

_____

_____

_____

_____

_____

_____

_____

10

Leadership Dilemmas
Ethical Challenges Can Make or Break a CEO

James Hackett
Chairman and Chief Executive Officer
Steelcase Inc.

Editors' Note: Behaving ethically is an every-day challenge. Preparation is critical. Steelcase CEO Jim Hackett practices for his big ethical dilemmas much the same way he practiced as a football player—by anticipating situations in advance and thinking through how he'll respond. This, he says, leads to better decisions when crises actually strike. The big events are most memorable: An unpopular and costly product recall ultimately reinforces the value of ethical behavior when it proves to be a factor in limiting the fire spread at the Pentagon on 9/11. But most ethical dilemmas in business are less dramatic, embedded in the nuts and bolts of daily decisions. Whether the issues are big or small, the real test is this: Are the ethical values underlying the decisions consistent and in keeping with the highest standards of both the organization and leader?

I am a CEO. Let that sink in for a moment.

Learning that a year ago, what's the first thing you might have wondered? How many stock options do I have?

Today, what's the first thing you think about? How many accounting problems? How good do you look in stripes?

What I'd like to be known for is integrity. And I know most people in business would like their CEOs to be known for integrity, too. They'd also like their CEO to perform, to help them reach their aspirations.

■ Your Roots Make Vivid Impressions

My father was a cattleman. His expertise was animal husbandry. And we had a long discussion once about when he went to buy cattle. He would look at the steer—from a distance, actually, because the buyers sat behind the fences—and the sellers would parade these animals in front of him and he had to decide instantaneously whether to bid on them. And so he developed an eye for this.

As I grew up, I tried to understand it. I couldn't imagine what he was seeing. I hadn't studied the science like he did. And I learned there was a lot of bull, literally, in the process of buying and selling animals. The big exercise was to avoid getting ripped off. Often he would say that you had to be sure to look at both sides of the animal, because they usually had an awful side and the sellers would only parade the good side in front of the buyers. I'll never forget that because it says something about perspective and 360-degree views for all issues.

One thing we don't want is to fall into the trap of being so highly principled that we can't think. We have to think around problems—all 360 degrees around them. We have to think around culture. We have to think around differences. And we have to think in terms of understanding what integrity is, then stand for it.

I was thirty-nine when I got this job, eight years ago. We were a family business at the time. We went public in February 1998. And the chairman, who was the single largest shareholder, talked a great deal about the chance to further the legacy of the company.

Steelcase had been highly successful—No. 1 in its business by a factor of two. We'd had a great legacy in terms of performance. My job was to not screw it up. As we were thinking about where Steelcase needed to go strategically, C. K. Prahalad called me one day and asked, "Would you do me a favor?" He said Bill Marriott, of hotel fame, was doing some similar work. In the early 1990s, the hotel industry—and Marriott was no exception—was reeling under the weight of real estate problems and a lack of tourism, trying to decide what to do with their business.

Steelcase had invested a lot in a venturing idea, to look at the fringes of our business to make it more exciting. I was quite intimidated because Mr. Marriott is an icon of many things—a family company with a sterling reputation for integrity and performance, strong Republican, knew a lot of the presidents personally.

The truth is, we hit it off. He liked the fact that I was young, trying to change an old family business—and he was old, trying to change an old family business.

We sat and talked a great deal about values. I'd been to Las Vegas a few times, I'd seen those massive new hotels going up and I noticed there was no Marriott hotel. Have you noticed? Vegas was the center of hotel building in the world in the early 1990s—and not one Marriott hotel.

I thought there's a simple idea for how to grow your business: Go into gambling.

One problem. Mr. Marriott is a Mormon, and hence, his philosophy about life and his value system suggested that wouldn't be a great thing.

Since then, Marriott bought the Ritz-Carlton chain, and they have invested in Las Vegas, but forty miles out in the desert, with no gambling. Bill Marriott proved that you can still stick to your values and win—even in Las Vegas.

■ The Peace of Knowing

Flying home, I thought of the peace that Mr. Marriott had— knowing what he needed to do. It was something that made me very jealous.

How could he make a decision to not invest in Las Vegas when all of his people, certainly his family members, were putting pressure on him to increase the performance of his business? And yet, he was at total peace.

Being thirty-nine years old, maybe six months into the job, you do not have a lot of peace as CEO. And it occurred to me that I wanted that peace. I wanted the opportunity to be able to make critical decisions and have the comfort of knowing that I had made the right decisions.

So that year I told our management team about Bill Marriott. I talked about airplanes having altitude and attitude indicators, which tell whether you're at the right height and whether you are level. So I asked, "What would tell me that I was pointing our company in the right direction," that I was still on the right (attitudinal) plane, as Mr. Marriott understood so clearly?

I needed to know right then how I would respond when I was faced with the same sort of big business dilemma. What am I gonna do?

Imagine this: The company's laying off sixty-six hundred people, our profits drop by 90 percent, we just lost the biggest job in the state of Michigan, and we find out that we have a flammability problem in one of our new products.

I thought maybe one day I'd be in a situation like that. What would I do?

I'm glad I prepared. Because a few years back, we created a new product line that is exceptional. The best way to describe it in the cubicle world, where panels form walls, is that at Steelcase we found that the surface of the panel and the surface on the wall could be interchanged, providing greater flexibility to our customers.

What we didn't know at the time was that the fire code also changed when the panel was placed on a wall—that the wall that surrounds you in a room has a stricter code than the cubicle wall. Even worse, all over the world, the codes are different. We had sold thousands of these interchangeable panels. But— when we learned of the fire code differences—faced with this flammability risk, we knew we had to do the right thing. We had not had one damaged installation. Our customers even called to tell us, "Oh, don't worry about it. What are you worried about, no one will ever have a problem."

We even had people inside the company say that just because they were sold as interchangeable, that didn't mean people would actually exchange the panels.

Back to my airplane trip, coming home from Bill Marriott. I wanted to know how I would act before I faced such a decision, because when all the pressure's on you to perform, the last thing you want to do is be searching for that attitude indicator. How are you going to act when you get in trouble? Because, I can guarantee you, in business, you will.

■ Steelcase Ethics and the Pentagon

It was over a year ago that we took that $40 million charge for the panel flammability problem. We recalled every panel, replaced it with a stricter fire code product. All our executives lost their bonuses that year. But we let the factory workers keep their bonuses, because they didn't contribute to the problem.

September 11, 2001, a jetliner crashed into a corner of the Pentagon. The product that was behind that wall was the new Steelcase fire code panel material.

That night, I remember thinking, first of all, about everything all of us were thinking about on that tragic day. But also, how good and how proud Steelcase could feel about having done everything it could to help people survive in that horrible setting.

In fact, we now know that the bomb blast didn't destroy the windows where the plane entered because they had just been reinforced. Given the amount of jet fuel, it incinerated all of our panel product that it touched. But the fire didn't spread because of our improved replacement panels.

And in five days we delivered brand new workstations for the fifteen hundred people who had been displaced.

I take a lot of pride in that story. But I'll tell you, when that charge for $40 million was going down, it wasn't so popular.

Think about that write-off decision. There was no one around. I couldn't tell anybody. I couldn't tell a board member. I couldn't tell a customer. I had to decide. Alone.

Imagine that you're in that setting and you've had the benefit of having talked with a Bill Marriott. Do you already know how you'll act? Or what decision you'll make? That's an exercise to think about and develop now.

What if you've grown up in a place where these values haven't been emphasized? How do you know that things are as they seem, or as you're told? What do you draw upon? You need to find out.

You need to learn about character and integrity. Search out people in your businesses who are noted for integrity. Somehow you'll find them. They won't always be at the top of the company. You want to find out how they wrestled their hardest ethical challenges to the ground. Learning that can give you the benefit of not having made a mistake—and yet you still get to learn from them, as they learned.

The formulaic value of integrity, knowing why it's important, does more than just build character—it actually allows you to lead.

Our chairman, Bob Hew, taught me this. He said you cannot be a leader if you don't have trust. And you can't have trust if you don't have integrity. He told me that ten years ago—before it was popular. In fact, at the time, going public was popular. And we talked about all the minutiae, all the fooling that was going on. Steelcase would come out every quarter with earnings as they were. And I'd get the crap beat out of me by the analysts. But my mentor at Steelcase said, "Don't listen to them, just do what's right."

He was right. The right way of doing things ended up surviving. In fact, now it's become law.

■ Ethics Have Become Prominent Again

That irony is that ethics are in again. In our science of studying how people work, we have found that in the sociology of the companies with the most innovative product development teams, trust is a key element in how well teams work together.

Makes common sense, doesn't it?

And when we diagnose the teams that break up and miss deadlines, trust is one of their biggest problems.

So our business is about trying to improve that sociology of trust. Steelcase has a vested interest, actually, in how leadership is built—because we think our facilities can enable that.

My football coach at Michigan, Bo Schembeckler, had a story I'll never forget. When he was growing up, his father was a fireman. And they had a test to get promoted. Bo's dad went to take this test in this little town in Ohio. And the guy Bo's dad was competing with cheated—and his dad wouldn't cheat.

The guy who cheated got a higher score and got the promotion.

So Bo came home from school one day and his father was dejected about losing this promotion. Bo learned that his father didn't cheat. And it had an indelible mark on him that—and this is why you've got to find that person in your life who can reach you this way—that he never wanted to succeed on the basis of cheating, either. The temptations in college athletics are immense. But Bo pounded that into us—we're not gonna cheat. We're gonna do it the right way. And I've had more pleasure in talking to Bo about how we're faced with these kinds of things today and how much he influenced me.

One consideration, as we go through this time in our business lives when power is abused, is to realize that most of the problem is a function of flawed integrity and flawed character.

It's also about people not understanding their leverage. I'm fond of saying that if you're an officer at Steelcase and you have to tell people that you are, you've failed. One of the things I look for and that I'd rather see leaders be more conscious of is how their power can be used for good. And they should do it actively and visibly.

The second thing is about learning that you're human, which means you'll be faced with situations, and have to know how you'll act when they come up.

The final thing is critical thinking. I suggested that seeing 360 degrees around you is a good starting basis for assessing problems. Critical thinking means being able to see below the issues and the problem. How many times has someone said, "If only I had thought how stupid that was."

It's because they didn't take the time to critically think and assess. That's a right no one can take away from you.

As Ken Blanchard once wrote, "There's no softer pillow than a clear conscience."

■ Teaching Through Your Stories

How do you prepare people for dealing with these types of issues? Storytelling is one of the best media for that. You can role-play through dilemmas forcing people to imagine themselves in a difficult situation and see how they handle it.

The most common problem you find as a CEO is that there are these huge paradoxes—and one way to think about problems in general is that the higher you are in the company, the more paradoxical the problems you face. Let's take an environmental issue. We have a machine that counts emissions, but somebody turned it off. We found out about it and self-reported to the state of Michigan. They fined us $500,000. Our people knew they were going to get a fine by telling the truth.

We go through those exercises all the time, believing that the shareholders have bought into the notion that we're a values-based company. So we would have lost that $500,000 anyway.

The reason you invest in our company is because we stand for those things. And this is why I urge our developing leaders to imagine being in that setting, making those trade-offs about reporting yourself for a violation. What are you going to do? You don't have to tell anybody. But if you don't tell the truth, it will come back to haunt you forever.

We often find ourselves in settings where it's not so black-and-white. We get into situations where the egos of people will be in conflict, where both can feel strongly that their idea is the right thing. It's very dangerous because you're into values. That's why I've added this element of critical thinking. You have to think through the problem as deeply as you can. You want that to be a shared responsibility. And the truth is, the candor is, the more mistakes you make, actually, the better people will learn. We want some of these errors to persist so that we can learn from them and actually get stronger.

That takes us to what we call morality. We had one case when the guy did not have a system of right and wrong in his head and he ripped the company off for millions of dollars because he thought that was OK. Now he lacked integrity. He never had the mentoring that I'm talking about—and that I got. He never had anyone say to him, "Imagine you're going to be in this situation, what will you do?" So one test is that as a CEO, your job is to leverage integrity.

Often we'll get into a situation and ask ourselves what are the ethics that we're operating by. You're in a situation where the values are very clear: We tell the truth, we treat each other with dignity and respect, we honor the commitments we made. But you also find yourself where the values aren't as clear, there's a problem you face. An example would be changing the pay of our factory workers to stay competitive. What's your ethic going to be on the extent you profit as an executive on the basis of their reduction in pay? As a management team, we said we can't profit on that, the ethic can't be that we end up benefiting. So the design of whatever you do has to work to benefit the whole, or it'll fall apart.

How are people assessed and valued? In their performance review, we ask how well we think they embody the values of the company. I can say in all candor that I often will reflect to my management team, "Let's look at how this person thinks." For me, as a CEO, always remember that I'm not going to be with many of these people but for a millisecond, and then may not see them for a year. But you can, in that short time, understand how they process information, how they evaluate issues, how they trade off consequences. So I look at how well people think through issues, what basis they have for reasoning things. And I'm most uncomfortable with it, because it puts me in this role that I am making judgments on people in a way that could enhance or break their career. So I have to be ethical about that. We have an open dialog about ethics, an open evaluation about values, reinforcing the need to think critically.

■ Explaining Leadership Perspectives

We have a weekly dialog with our employees over the Internet via e-mail, and I talk quite candidly about these and other issues. I try to reason out loud for them on a range of perspectives. That's the best you can do.

Remember what I said about CEOs' getting paid a lot of money to solve dilemmas—the higher you are in the company, the more paradoxical the problems that you have to solve. The bend-but-don't-break notion is a great one. But if you process that incorrectly, you can forever seal the notion that you're a risk-taker with something that shouldn't be risk-takeable.

If it were a binary system, where I could give you the inputs that say you get this close to the line and a signal will go off, then we don't need you to make decisions. So as a leader, you've got to see this as a reason for your being, which is to understand dilemmas, to reason them through, to talk them through.

I hearken back to mentoring, because if you don't have the influence of someone who's been there, you'll likely not understand the edges, because you can rationalize things too easily.

We have a big debate about whether people should be drawn and quartered if they screw up. Isn't the best evidence of a screw-up a post in the ground and somebody's head sticking on it?

I don't believe so. People lose their job at Steelcase for doing the wrong thing, no question, but I think making examples of them is a cheap way to motivate people. The more valuable and difficult way is to reach people in another way, without fear being the only motivator.

We show our constituents and shareholders what the company stands for. I'm worried about businesses' obsession with profit at any cost. I'm worried that leaders at Steelcase one day might feel the pressure to perform means that we have to give up values.

When I played football in a Michigan program that didn't cheat, we had the best record in college football in those four years. I didn't win any bowl games, unfortunately, but we knew success. I work for a company that when we went public, the investment banker and I got in a big fight. I said, "You can't tell those people we're going to grow 15 percent per year." Warren Buffett says trees don't grow to the sky. Eventually, you're going to hit a wall. So we had a three-year projection and it was good the first year and it softened the second. We got beaten down for that limitation because there was so much emphasis on top-line growth, to the exclusion of all else. If you go back and look at the performance now, it looks pretty good, but we didn't want to overpromise beforehand.

How many of you should worry about changing the company when the values are wrong? Is this a crusade that you want to take on?

That happened in our business, where somebody spoke up because they were so upset. We know what happened at Enron.

If you see one thing going wrong, you can deal with it. If you see two or three things going wrong, you start to look for a pattern or ask if these are just bad eggs in the basket. Don't compromise the fact of what you see: It either is or it isn't, it's either a bad case or a good case. Be certain about that.

■ It Takes Courage to Act

The decision to act is much more difficult. As you enter an enterprise, take some time to understand what's going on. Don't give up on your values. Make an effort to talk to people and say, "Are you seeing this, or am I missing it?" If they say, "You don't understand, that's the way things are done around here," that should set off an alarm in your head. Eventually most everyone will get an opportunity to talk to someone near the top and they'll hopefully ask what you think. People like me value people who can see things in a broad perspective. And we get concerned when there's activism in the corporation on a singular issue.

This is another thing that takes judgment, wisdom, and conviction. You understand right now that you're going to be faced with dilemmas in a company and the boss is the one that you're worried about telling. How are you going to act?

I already know how I'm going to act if a board member acts that way, because I've had to think about it. There's a right way to handle that and a wrong way—and the right way is to not compromise what you stand for.

At Steelcase, we have a rule that when a secretary might shift and work for me for a while, I say to them, "If I ever tell you to lie, you tell me no." If you worked at Steelcase, we would tell you this when you first started. Understand what we stand for—you have to buy into this and then have the courage to live up to it.

I've been with Steelcase twenty-one years. One of my jobs was managing a sales area. We often find several dealers will be chasing the same customers, creating conflict.

There was one incident in which I lost business for an honest dealer by my own misstep and then, when confronted, didn't own up to it. I was forever stressed by that decision, because I realize that I can't have trust if I don't have integrity. And this dealer—it took a long time, because he knew I had done it—well, eventually I had to tell him the story. I had to go to confession and say, "I screwed up, I did this wrong, and I told you the wrong thing, because I didn't want to fail in your eyes. I was new, will you forgive me?" He did. And we've been great friends ever since.

■ Balance Honesty, Candor, Judgment

It's a never-ending challenge to make sure that mix of honesty and candor and judgment are in equilibrium. You must have a sense, when you're in a job like mine, when that's out of balance—you can see a pattern. While spiritual guides can be great lessons, this part of business requires that you have interaction with mentors and people who have been there.

I believe, in the face of everything that you've seen in the paper or the companies you've worked for, that by and large business does more good than harm. And leadership comes from trust and integrity. One great thing about being human is that each day you can start anew. The past can be the point at which you didn't understand and the next day can be the day that you did understand—and people can change.

But these dilemmas are always around.

We bought a company in Europe that was doing business in Russia, and the only way you could get furniture in was to pay off the tariff people so that the product could move through on time for your customer. We stopped the practice. I don't hold that as an example of how great we are. There's just no room for violating our values.

What happens over time is that you will either survive in terms of the business, or you can't do business there—because the ethics are so poor. There's no such thing as, "We got the business, and we had to compromise ourselves." That's not a state you're allowed at Steelcase.

The Greek philosophers already debated the "end justifies the means" question long before we had to deal with it. And it doesn't. It doesn't because your life is a series of these actions that get replayed in terms of the effect that you created. So if you helped orphanages, brought food to people, and did things that made good, but you had to cheat to do it, it takes away the magic of what you were able to accomplish.

At Steelcase, the way you learn about ethics is when you're expressing your view—as I did one day—and one of these people gave me the finger, because they thought that I was so off track in my thinking. But they felt comfortable enough to do that. And that's the culture in our company, where the CEO has to be approachable when people disagree.

And it is hard. I'll tell you, I want to use power every time I can to squash it. But, in fact, it makes me better with an environment that open. It's more complicated when you're in a part of the world where you can't imagine their culture. Say a female executive and I, as part of our global business practices, show up at the border of Saudi Arabia. They say, "I'm sorry, she can't enter." We have a plant there. What are we supposed to do?

Now, to some, this is not an immoral thing, or doesn't lack integrity. It's a values issue in the sense of one's beliefs about diversity. But we made a decision to do business in their land and should be prepared to honor Saudi traditions and mores, as part of that decision, to the extent our own corporate values permit.

At Steelcase, we don't have to do things that are immoral. In fact, in Saudi you can't bring in liquor or anything that would be deemed pornographic, and there's "no interest" in their banking system. But when we built a factory there, we had to pay a fee to the government that was not a bribe—this went through an audit process—but was a form of interest for a government loan. But they didn't have to call it that.

■ Candid Role-Plays Help in Decisions

You actually have to role-play through these things to understand what they really are. Let's be quite candid. What is really going on here? And when you find out, would you tell your mother?

"This really isn't a bribe, mom, we just slip them beer so we can get the stuff to the poor kids."

Your mother always has a way of saying, "Come on, that's a bribe." Think about the influence someone like that has in your life.

These dilemmas, by the way, aren't bad. You can make a lot of money if that's important, or have a lot of prestige if you learn how to solve dilemmas. Anyone can cheat to solve the dilemma, it takes somebody special to solve this problem through other methods—such as persuasion.

As we expand globally, I'll go to meet the government, we'll ask them to come visit us—maybe we'll invest more. All kinds of things can happen. You may shake your head, but it works.

Remember the book, *The Ugly American,* the notion that we influence, by our own value system, places around the world that aren't ready for us. I'm very sensitive to that—but at the same time know when it's over the line, cheating to get your way.

You can find similar kinds of situations—say you found a German partner that had committed atrocities, or an American company that had used slavery way back in history. How far do you let those long-distant issues drive your sensibilities about their value set today?

We need to look people in the eye and say, "How do you feel about this?" And when I get comfort that they understand things the way I do, then we do business. You know, we trust, we have integrity. But when they don't, or I'm suspicious, we walk away from those situations.

Take the wall panel flammability problem. The way I found out about it was because somebody hadn't reported it to their boss, because they were afraid the boss would squash it. So I assigned somebody on the side to go in and investigate—and it wasn't a very popular thing.

Say you had a lot of integrity, and someone came in and said, "Now, I want to talk to you about what's going on here with this fire code." And you responded, "I took care of it." They walked through hours of such discussions about it, like doing an audit. And we got to the truth. We found out what had happened. And we had to fire some people.

So it became an important story.

■ Stories Best Reinforce Integrity

Stories do more to teach integrity in our company than anything. Some people had to leave, other people got reassigned, and the people who spoke up got lauded. Some people didn't want to tell me, didn't want to tell the boss. That goes on a lot. The leverage, the power that this executive had was overarching in terms of intimidation, such that people were afraid to give him bad news.

Don't let that happen to you. The thing is, I knew better—that in this situation, this was somebody who tended to use their power to leverage in a negative way. So why was I not surprised that this happened? I learned a very valuable lesson five years ago.

Jeff Immelt uses a word that I like to use, too—*literacy*. Literacy is the knowledge of reading—the ability to—read—but it's also the knowledge of a topic, and so there's an illiteracy in boardrooms and with CEOs about lots of topics. Environmental issues are one area where people suffer from not having the right background.

Do you know what polyvinyl chloride, PVC, is and why it's a really dangerous substance? The chemistry of that is something that most boardrooms wouldn't understand. So we talk in terms of improving our literacy on topics like that.

I think there are about seven thousand pages now in the accounting code, so there's a fair amount of discretion in the way you treat something. Now, the literacy at all levels of a company of those seven thousand pages is probably uneven, and probably worse in most cases where there's fraud.

Was Ken Lay a victim of his own illiteracy, or of his lack of values? I don't want to sit in judgment of someone else, because I could be there myself someday—particularly if I'm illiterate or I just didn't know—if I made a dumb bonehead decision.

The commitment we make is that we try to improve our literacy on topics that we don't understand. So we have a big environmental, intense system of explanation going on right now about the chemistry of our products, and the use of technology.

What the CEOs that are honest are worried about is that there's a fair amount of discretion—such as when they say, "Jim, you know, you took that charge last quarter versus this quarter. You just cheated."

No, I didn't at all. I applied the rules. The pendulum has to swing in an even way, I think. That's when integrity becomes a big deal.

When you become a CEO of a big company, Steve Forbes hosts you in his apartment in New York.

Eight years ago I sat there with him at lunch. Al Dunlap was leaving Scott Paper for Sunbeam—and I remember feeling offended by the notion that I had to start in my job as CEO and fire people. And I said, "You know, Steve, why don't you write an article about people who've laid off all these workers, and then they added them back, you know, how many years does it take to come back."

And he wrote—and quoted me—and said, "Jim Hackett never wants to tell his mother that he's laid off anybody," which is something I said. But this year I had to lay off sixty-six hundred people, the first time in eight years. We've had a huge difficult time struggling in the way we've rationalized it, but I feel it's a failure of our ability to see the wave of problems coming. On the other side, I don't know that we could have avoided it. Our industry has been hammered by a 40 percent decline in volume in twelve months—and it's just never happened before.

■ Communicating the Realities

I think the most important thing is to communicate the realities of the business to the employees. We've been very open about that. We've done everything we possibly could to avoid layoffs. Early in the process, when we could see what was happening, we let people take voluntary leaves of absence, we tried to do anything to avoid the layoffs. And—because most of our employees are factory workers—seniority guides the layoffs. So we tried to keep younger people working if we could, if older people decided to take some time off.

But at some point the reality hits: We had to shrink the business to keep it profitable and maintain a sustainable workplace with a balance of the people. I think that's understood. Does it make people a little nervous? Sure. Does it make them feel uncertain about their own position? Yes. We worked very hard to be sure that people left the company with as much of their self-esteem as possible—with an ability to reconnect in their next job intact.

I'll share a mistake we made twelve years ago, which was almost as long ago as we had any prior layoffs. It was a very small number, 150 people, but at that point some were concerned that they not "take anything confidential" with them. So after we told one woman that we no longer had work for her, we had a protection services person "help" her to her car.

The message that sent in the organization was horrible—because we took a person who had been a valued colleague, who sat next to you for fifteen years, and in your mind she suddenly became a criminal.

So this time we said, "No protection service people, nobody, you know, with a gun helping people to the car," because we remembered that woman.

When you think about it, if she was somebody that we didn't trust, she should have been gone a long time ago. If she's somebody that we couldn't have trusted, she's already taken what she wants. We need to send a message to the rest of the company that this is the condition of business, and not disrespect those who are leaving. And that helped a very difficult message be better accepted this time.

Here's another: I got a call one Sunday a couple of hours after midnight. The guy was drunk. He worked in one of our factories. He said, "Jim, this is so-and-so." And I said, "You know what time it is—2:30 in the morning?" He goes, "Yeah, I figure that the executives of Steelcase like a beer every now and then, and I just had a few beers, and I want to talk to you." My number is in the phone book. And I said, "Well, if you want to come and see me Monday, I'll move things around for you. But it's 2:30 in the morning. I'm not gonna talk to you." We went on for fifteen minutes and I finally had to hang up on him. He was not coherent.

On Sunday, I called our security folks and said, "I'm worried about this guy." They went to his house. He had killed himself.

That was six years ago. My family got to see that play out. My kids were younger. One said, "Dad, why would somebody kill himself? You didn't talk to him. Maybe you could have stopped it." I had a lot of guilt about that, because I didn't recognize he was in so much trouble. I didn't know his history—he had depression problems.

■ Walk in Their Shoes to Know What They Think

But forever this taught me that no matter what you think you're communicating and getting through, you've got to imagine what others are trying to get through. So a year ago we started meeting with everybody—and I would talk to the plants constantly about business conditions and help them understand. They still write me some hate mail. And I write them back—in fact said, "If you sign your name, you're proving to me that you have courage." But I still got a lot of anonymous letters. So I wrote to the whole company and said, "If you have any courage, then you should sign your name—and I promise you won't get in trouble."

So now, everybody signs their name. They write me the nastiest letters during this tough time. My wife says, "Why are you reading that before you go to bed at night?" That's when I do my e-mail. It's hard to sleep after reading some—people have breast cancer, they can't get to the doctor, the kids are sick.

Now, you won't read about these things in the business press. But that's what it's like to be a CEO, dealing with those kinds of issues. The bulk of it is about people. Can I use the leverage of my power for good? Can I help that person with breast cancer who lost her job? Can we give them the loan? Can we do something to help them in some way?

I didn't invent that Steelcase culture, that's the way I grew up in the company. And I'm passing that on. Someday, when you'll be leaders, you will want to remember that you can use the power of your office to do good for people.

I believe people are good. But I believe that for a few in business, the focus got off track, greed overwhelmed them. Imagine yourself being worth a billion dollars in two years.

I remember Warren Buffett saying, "This is a mirage, it's not worth it, it can't be real, there's no value, they weren't making money." At Steelcase, we had made $250 million, went public, made $270 million the next year—and the share prices went down. I couldn't understand it. And yet, a company that was not making any money saw its share price double.

What do you want to do with your life? I think the pendulum is swinging back to where people want to be known as ethical. Many people will talk about it for years, but the only way to judge their worth has been in how many options they had, how much money they made.

Maybe we can get lucky—and begin to judge people by how much good they do from their position, too. Wouldn't that be a great signature? You'll still make enough money to serve you and your family forever, even without the extraordinary pay.

I'm hoping that the wave of using this leverage for good comes back. And you know, I don't have that many more years doing this—and I don't want to leave in a period when people have disrespect for the job that we're supposed to do.

The question is, can you change—change the world, change your company, change people? That's the proverbial thing for you to think about: What do you want to do and be as a leader?

Exercises in Ethics

Your company may one day have to deal with its own version of the awful scenario suggested by Jim Hackett. In the context of your own business, imagine having to deal with the following set of situations:

- Your profits are down 90 percent.
- You just lost your biggest potential sale of the year.
- Now you must lay off thousands.
- And a major quality problem has just surfaced.

1. What do you do about the quality problem? Hackett says it's too late to figure out how you'll handle such crises when they hit—and far better to prepare in advance so you'll know how you will respond, should the time come. With that in mind, write what you would want to do about the quality problem in your company's version of Hackett's scenario.

_____

_____

_____

_____

_____

_____

_____

_____

_____

_____

_____

_____

_____

_____

_____

_____

_____

_____

2. How could this example—or an actual horror story that has already
taken place in your company or industry—be incorporated to add
value and focus to your Teachable Point of View on business ethics?

_____

_____

_____

_____

_____

_____

_____

_____

_____

_____

_____

_____

_____

_____

_____

_____

_____

_____

_____

_____

_____

_____

_____

_____

_____

_____

_____

_____

11

Ethics and Fundamental Decisions

The Internally Directed and Other-Focused Mindset

Robert Quinn
*Professor of Organizational Behavior
and Human Resource Management
University of Michigan Business School*

Editors' Note: The tug to conform to organizational norms can breed conflict between doing what is "ethically right" and doing what the company sees as normal and expected. Even when deviance is tolerated by a firm in the spirit of transformational change, almost immediately natural organizational forces set out to harness that unusual behavior and force it back within the norms. Organizational life becomes reduced to a series of expected "transactions"—and those among us who think they behave with high ethical standards can become little more than hypocritical conformists. Professor Quinn provides rich examples of how these competing mindsets can unwittingly conspire to undermine a leader's ethical behavior. Understanding the power of these forces is critical to consciously deciding when to succumb to their influences— and when to stand firm against them.

I n describing his ethical dilemmas, Steelcase CEO Jim Hackett told a story about a defect in one of his products. The corporate financial picture was not very positive and recalling the product would put even more pressure on the financials. To complicate things further, some of his customers indicated that they were not troubled by the defect. Yet, after considerable wrestling, Hackett decided to recall the product.

After he described his dilemma, MBA students did a debrief, focusing on Hackett's decision. Some challenged the story. Some argued that if the financial situation had been worse he would not have made the decision to do the recall. It would have cost him his job.

Here the students touch a key question: Do you do the right thing when your own survival hangs in the balance?

■ The Normal Mindset

Normal thinking says you do what you must to survive. Survival is the first law of nature. Everyone follows it. Everyone should follow it. This is the core of the *transactional mindset*.

Most people spend most of their time in a transactional mindset. What this means is that they are self-focused but driven by external forces. This is true even of people in positions of authority.

■ The Alternative Mindset

There is an alternative mindset. In it, people become directed by internal forces and focused on others, and the first law of nature falls away. Something is more important than survival. In this *transformational mindset,* the more important thing is the ability to unleash potential.

In the transactional mindset, we are attempting to preserve equilibrium. We are seeking to stay inside our own comfort zone. We are even willing to distort reality to fool ourselves into believing that we are in control. Indeed, it is normal for all of us to prefer to preserve the illusion of control rather than face the challenge of effectiveness. Given the choice between being in control or being effective, we choose being in control. Being effective means that we must be in touch with changing reality and be willing to change with it. It requires the monitoring of our own hypocrisy and the willingness to close our own hypocrisy gaps.

In considering the two mindsets, I would like to illustrate three points:

- First, hypocrisy is ubiquitous. We all lack integrity. This includes the author and the reader.
- Second, the world conspires to lure us toward mediocrity and transactional thinking.
- Third, making fundamental decisions about our own identity means we close our integrity gaps and we enter an alternative transformational mindset where we become empowered and empowering to others.

Hypocrisy Is Ubiquitous

Some years ago, I was invited to a meeting of senior officers at one of the military academies. The officer in charge talked at length about the moral decay in society. There seemed to be no focus to his discussion, and I could not figure out what problem was actually concerning these men. Eventually it was revealed that some of the students at the academy had been caught cheating on their exams. The cadets were not following the academy's honor system. The officers' explanation for the cadets' behavior was corruption in society. They felt that by the time an eighteen-year-old arrived at the academy it was too late; the cadet was irredeemable.

After a long discussion about the corruption in society, I attempted to turn the topic around. I asked if anyone in the room had served in Vietnam. Most had. I asked if any of them had participated in the phenomenon known as the body count—a measurement system used to determine how American forces were performing in which, at the end of each battle, the number of enemy dead were counted, and the number reported. As this process unfolded, vastly exaggerated numbers were routinely reported.

From the atmosphere of discomfort in the room, it was clear that some had participated. Why, I asked, would an officer and a gentleman (as opposed to a noncommissioned cadet) engage in such behavior? Answering my own question, I suggested that when an impossible objective is given to people in a large hierarchy and when it is accompanied by immense pressure to produce, the people in the organization will also experience growing pressure to engage in unethical behavior. An invisible form of corruption at the top, the exercise of authority without concern or demand without support, results in a very visible form of corruption at the bottom.

I then suggested that perhaps the problem with the cadets did not have its roots "out there" in society. Maybe large numbers of students were cheating because the system demanded they cheat and taught them to do so. Were the arrangement of classes, the design of assignments and workloads, and traditional military values like "cooperate and graduate" combining to teach, require, and reward cheating? Was the problem in the cadets alone, or was it in the relationship between the cadets and the authority figures who were condemning and externalizing the problem?

There was a long silence. Finally, the man in charge spoke. He turned to the man next to him and, as if I had never said a word, resumed the old discussion about the moral decay in society. For the rest of the day they ignored me—I simply did not exist.

This is not a story just about the military. It is a story about every organization and every human being. We all lack the courage to engage a reality that is calling on us to live with accountability and to make deep change. We are all hypocrites most of the time. We are all the Enron executives that we love to condemn.

The Lure to Transactional Mediocrity

While I was once making a presentation at a large company, a man in the audience raised his hand and identified himself as being from a particular plant. I knew the plant well. Historically, it had been a place of poor performance and continual unrest. Everything about the place was bad. Then a complete turnaround took place. Management moved from the traditional assumptions of control and distrust to concepts of teamwork and cooperation. Nearly every practice and procedure shifted dramatically. After considerable effort and pain, the change paid off. The plant reached levels of performance that led not only the company but the industry. It became nationally known for high-quality performance.

This man seemed very proud of the company's accom-
plishments and his role in the turnaround. This day, however,
he appeared tired. He inquired, "How do you empower people
when the corporation does everything it can to kill innovative
efforts?" I asked him to explain. He argued that the company
was not particularly interested in high performance and, in fact,
did everything it could to discourage it. I asked him for an example, and he told the following story:

> Last week, we had a crisis on the shop floor. People from all
> over the plant willingly pitched in to confront and resolve the
> problem. Many people worked for over thirty hours straight.
> At one point, everyone was hungry, so the plant manager or-
> dered pizza for everybody. The next week, I was sitting in the
> plant manager's office when the finance guy walked in. He
> threw down a piece of paper and said, "I'm not paying this."
> The plant manager picked up the piece of paper and became
> red-faced as he noted that it was the receipt for the pizza. He
> crushed it into a ball, handed it to the finance guy, and said,
> "You can do one of two things. You can pay this, or you can put
> it 'where the sun don't shine,' but I don't want to see it again."

He pointed out that this was just one of many small examples of corporate resistance to the innovative team approach.
When he finished, I clarified his original question: "What you're
telling me is that you have developed a highly innovative,
highly successful plant that is different from other plants in the
corporation. You're regularly confronted by pressure to conform
to rules and regulations that could cause you to become an ordinary plant. The corporation keeps trying to wear you and your
colleagues down, to make you ordinary, like the other plants."

He agreed that I understood the issue. I told him that I had
an absolute answer to his problem—he should quit. I instructed
him to return to the plant and tell his colleagues to stop trying,

to give up. Give the company what it wants: Become like the other plants.

He said that my advice was crazy. In reply, I asked him why he and his colleagues were trying so hard to maintain an excellent plant. He thought about it for a while. Finally he said, "Because it's the right thing to do."

I said, "You seem to be very proud of what you're doing. There appears to be a high level of satisfaction in achieving excellence. There also seems to be a great deal of pain involved. Every day you meet some form of resistance, some force that would wear you down." He agreed.

I continued, "It seems to me that you have to be clear about something. Excellence is a form of deviance. If you perform beyond the norms, you disrupt all the existing control systems. Those systems will then alter and begin to work to routinize your efforts. That is, the systems will adjust and try to make you normal. The way to achieve and maintain excellence is to deviate from the norm. You become excellent because you are doing things normal people do not want to do. You become excellent by choosing a path that is risky and painful, a path that is not appealing to others. The question is, why would anyone ever want to do something painful?

"You have already answered this question. You do it because it's right and because it brings enormous internal satisfaction. That is the key. That's why I suggested that you consider giving up. If giving up becomes a serious option, it suggests that the external punishment is beginning to outweigh the internal satisfaction. We need to recognize that external punishment is a natural process that is never going to end. It forces us to weigh the trade-offs between internal satisfaction and external punishment. Usually this kind of contemplation supplies us with the strength to continue confronting the resistance."

The point is that all systems regress to the mean. If we choose to live by a higher principle, any higher principle, the system will work to drive us back to mediocrity. Excellence is a function of living in the transformational and not the transactional mindset.

A Fundamental Choice Can Alter What You See

The term "fundamental choice" comes from the work of Robert Fritz. He tells us that a fundamental choice has to do with our state of being or our basic life orientation. It is a choice to live in a given way. It is different from what he calls primary and secondary choices. Primary choices are about specific results. Secondary choices are about the means to achieve the results. Normally we focus on the latter two. We, for example, might commit to increase quality in the company (primary choice). We are going to do this by introducing a new program like Six Sigma (secondary choice). We tend not to focus on making a fundamental decision, saying, "I am going to live the principles of quality in every aspect of my personal and professional life."

In *The Path of Least Resistance,* Fritz writes:

> There are many people who have chosen the religious path (primary choice), without making the fundamental choice to live in accordance with their highest spiritual truths. There are many people who have chosen to be married (primary choice), without making the fundamental choice to live from within a committed relationship. . . . Fundamental choices are not subject to changes in internal or external circumstances. If you make the fundamental choice to be true to yourself, then you will act in ways that are true to yourself whether you feel inspired or depressed, whether you feel fulfilled or frustrated, whether you are at home, at work, with your friends, or with your enemies. . . . When you make a fundamental choice, convenience and comfort are not ever at issue, for you always take action based on what is consistent with your fundamental choice [p. 193].

Fundamental decisions lead us to act with authentic engagement, a characteristic of the transformational being state. Authentic engagement means we are authentic and engaged. To be authentic is to be genuine, actual, legitimate, true, real, pure, and uncorrupted. We become authentic by being "true to what is highest" in us. We do this by committing to live by principle, to do what is right when it is not pleasurable. Normal or natural people live by fleeing pain and pursuing pleasure. It is unnatural to do otherwise. Yet when we make fundamental commitments we are choosing to be unnatural. We choose, in certain circumstances, to embrace pain and flee pleasure. We make sacrifices for others. We become extraordinary.

The decision to increase our authenticity while remaining engaged has profound impacts. Note the sentence, "When people make a fundamental choice to be true to what is highest in them, or when they make a choice to fulfill a purpose in their life, they can easily accomplish many changes that seemed impossible or improbable in the past." Consider the illustration.

I remember a man—I'll call him Garret—who attended my Leading Change course in the Executive Education Program at the Michigan Business School. He was a company president. During the first three days of the course, he said very little. On Thursday morning, he asked if we might have lunch together and I agreed. Over lunch he told me that if he had attended my course any time in the last five years, he would have been wasting his time. He had successfully turned around two companies and felt he knew everything there was to know about leading change.

Today, he told me, he was a lot more humble. There were five companies in his corporation. He had turned two of them around and was seen as the shining star among the presidents. He had earned the right to lead the largest company in the corporation. The current president of that largest company still had, however, eighteen months left until retirement. In the meantime,

Garret had been asked to try his hand at one more turnaround. The corporation had one company that was considered hopeless. It had once commanded a large market share for its product. Today, it had only a small percentage of the market and was still shrinking. Nobody believed this company could be turned around, so if Garret failed in his efforts, no one would hold it against him.

It had now been twelve months since he took on the challenge. He felt defeated. Everything that had worked for him before, everything his past had taught him, failed in the present situation. Morale was dismal. The numbers were dismal. The outlook for the future was dismal.

I asked Garret what he thought he would do next. On a paper napkin he listed his short-term objectives. He began to draw an organizational chart. He described the people in each of the senior positions and described the assignments or changes he was going to make in regard to each person on the chart. I found his answer unexciting. There was no commitment or passion in what he was telling me. Yet it was clear that Garret was a man of character with a sincere desire to succeed. I took a deep breath and asked a hard question.

"What would happen if you went back and told those people the truth? Suppose you told them that you have been assigned as a caretaker for a year and a half. No one believes the company can succeed and no one really expects you to succeed. You have been promised the presidency of the largest company, and the plan is to put you into the plum job. Tell them that you have, however, made a fundamental choice. You have decided to give up that plum job. Instead, you are going to stay with them. You are going to bet your career on them and you invite them to commit all the energy and goodwill they can muster into making the company succeed."

I was worried that I might have offended Garret. I half expected an angry response. He looked at me for a moment, then it was his turn to take a deep breath. To my surprise and relief, he said, "That is pretty much what I have been thinking." He paused, and in that moment I watched him make the fundamental decision. Almost immediately, he picked up the napkin and started doing a reanalysis. He said, "If I am going to stay, then this person will have to go; this person will have to be moved over here; and this person. . . ."

As he talked, there was now an air of excitement in Garret's words. Once he had made the fundamental decision to stay, everything changed. His earlier plans to move on to the larger company were suddenly scrapped. Garret had made a fundamental choice, and now he had a new life stance, a new outlook, and a new way to behave. The organization chart that made sense a few moments before now made no sense at all. None of the original problems had changed, but Garret had—and this made all the difference in the world.

■ Summary

The MBA students were asking an unanswerable question. We will never know what Jim Hackett would have done if the financial situation had been worse. Yet in asking that question they do us a service. They surface the key question. Do we live in the normal transactional state or the extraordinary transformational state?

It is normal for us to all spend most of our time in the first. In that state, we are externally driven and self-focused. In that state, survival is the first law of nature. We can, however, make fundamental decisions. When we do, we experience a dramatic change in outlook and we behave in abnormal ways. We become empowered and empowering because we are internally driven and other-focused. At such times, we make the product recall no matter how bad the financials.

The challenge is for all of us to see the hypocrisy that resides in us and to be in a continual state of closing our integrity gaps. It is then that we can find the transformational power to lead.

Exercises in Ethics

Think about a major challenge or question currently facing your business. Quinn helps make us aware of the multiple mindsets with which we make decisions.

1. What would be the normal Transactional Mindset—self-focused and externally driven (preserving the equilibrium, staying inside your comfort zone)—response to your business challenge?

_____

_____

_____

2. What could be a response option to your business challenge if you were to apply the transformational Alternative Mindset— other-focused and internally driven—doing the "right thing" even if it might be contrary to tradition?

_____

_____

_____

3. Which mindset choice would provide the better platform to represent your firm's commitment to integrity and business ethics?

_____

_____

_____

4. How could choosing the option you described in question 3 be incorporated in and enhance your Teachable Point of View on business ethics?

_____

_____

_____

12

Superstar Entrepreneur Meets Today's High-Bar Ethics

How Trilogy Is a Very Different Software Company

Joe Liemandt
Founder and Chief Executive Officer
Trilogy Software Inc.

Editors' Note: Times change and so do standards of business. Software entrepreneur Joe Liemandt examines the evolution of the times and his own company. Values take on growing importance as an organization matures. Initially, as an entrepreneurial start-up, Trilogy's values were around surviving long enough to develop its product. Now, it is focused on retaining customers by delivering the solutions they expect. So the little software company that once took a certain pride in its self-centeredness today has evolved into a deeply customer-focused organization. The changes were necessary, but not painless.

I started my business in the decade that culminated in the dot-com world. It's a very different world today.

During the dot-com boom, a lot of people forgot that if you don't have the right core values, if you don't have integrity and trust, the rest of the system falls apart. It really is a completely different world today. Trust in the free enterprise system—integrity, ethics, all of those issues—couldn't be more important than they are today.

Trilogy's journey started with five kids in the garage with a great idea.

Back then—in the early 1990s—raising venture capital supposedly wasn't hard. There were VC firms next to VC firms all along Sand Hill Road—right down the street from Stanford. The first time we went out and presented to raise money, the venture capitalist said, "Well, the number one thing that really matters is that you have an experienced management team." We were seniors at Stanford. We looked at each other. I jumped in, "I ran the cafeteria for a while." That didn't work. So that VC firm decided not to give us any money.

We regrouped and got the presentation geared up for the second time with another Sand Hill Road VC firm, starting it with a slide that said, "We don't have an experienced management team." Get that right out of the way, confront your weakness.

Their response: "It's true, we don't *always* need experienced management teams. We'll fund really great proven technologies." Proven performers who'd built the technology before? We didn't have a product yet, but tried explaining to them how we could do it.

The VC said, "You guys are from Stanford. I know the head of the CS department at Stanford. I'll just call him up to see what he thinks of your idea."

We knew: "He thinks it's never going to work," we said. They didn't give us money, either.

Third time's the charm, right? This time we picked a VC who's a Stanford graduate—and I think he felt sorry for us— no experienced management team and no radically improved technology.

He said, "Well, the third thing we look for, if you don't have the first two, is we'll sometimes fund a hit product, something that's like a game, or some little utility where, if the product hits, it hits—and we'll throw a little money that way just to see if it works."

He talked about, for example, a screensaver company that had flying toasters going across the screen.

But then he said, "The thing we won't do with hit products is try to sell Fortune 500 companies mission critical software."

Our next slide—in the middle of this presentation—said that not only were we selling mission critical software to the Fortune 500, but we were going to set a new high-end price point.

What would you do? Advance to the next slide? Or just turn the projector off and walk out?

Just to show them that we had a reason for walking out, we advanced to the next slide. And we never got funding there, either.

■ We Literally Lived in a Garage

We weren't giving up on our idea. This was the early nineties, and they were just starting to direct-mail credit cards to college graduates. So we went home and applied for some, figuring, "We'll just fund this baby on cash advances."

That's actually how we got the company funded. And we did a lot of these advances—for though we felt that we could build our new software product in a year, it ended up taking us three and a half years. And all this time, we literally were living in a garage. Our marketing plan was really simple: Build this thing that everybody says is impossible—everybody'll buy it.

For over three years we toiled away. Nobody really believed that we'd finish it or that it would work.

When we started, all our friends were very supportive. They'd say, "Great idea, this'll be really cool. Why don't you guys go do that?"

Our parents? Not so supportive. "You're dropping out of school? How far are you supposed to be from getting a degree? What's going on?"

I learned that if it actually takes you three and a half years to finish when you keep telling everybody it will take one year, then even your friends start to question you.

"Maybe you're not so good at this, Joe. Maybe you have no idea what you're doing. How long are you going to keep doing this?"

■ New High-End Price Point

Luckily for us, the product worked. We shipped it. Hewlett-Packard gave us millions for it. Then every major computer and telecommunication company purchased it. The rest was history. We were growing like crazy. Our pricing mechanism was, "This thing's worth a lot, so let's charge for it." And we set new high-end points.

As we started to become a big, real company, our view of what our job was didn't change—this garage mentality, build the product, set out the specifications, and make it the best product you've ever seen. We were very engineering oriented. For years, we just kept doing that—building great product and shipping it to our customers.

We were winning awards. *InfoWorld Magazine* gave us its product of the year award. Windows, Excel, and Word—all those products had won historically—and in the mid-1990s, we won it. We built the best products in the world. Things were going great.

And one of the things we loved about the enterprise software business was that if you had a product that works, it could just print money. You send customers a disk, they send you $25 million back. So we were throwing off cash.

Things were going great. Then, all of a sudden, the dot-com craze hits. So Trilogy decided, "Let's take a bunch of this cash and fund lots of dot-coms." Some of them worked. Some of them didn't. And some wasted a ton of money.

What next?

■ Most Global Enterprise Projects Fail

One of the problems with the enterprise software business is that while our product worked according to specification—contractual specification—the ability of our customers to actually garner value out of it was very low. The approach was, "Here's the contract, take the software, and good luck. You know, figure it out. Do whatever you want with it." In the enterprise software business, any expert will tell you that somewhere between 50 percent and 80 percent of Fortune 500 global projects fail.

On the cover of the *Wall Street Journal* every few months there's some article about another failure in enterprise software—some big write-off. There's been Nike, Whirlpool, Hershey. Two years ago, there wasn't enough chocolate for Halloween, because they were putting in a big ERP system and it didn't work.

That is not the exception. That is status quo. The stuff just doesn't work most of the time. And it leads to a business model where you sell it, it works according to spec, and then—a couple of years later—the customers say, "I didn't get anything for this."

We'd respond, "Well, it works, the product works. . . . If you look at the contract, it says here are the specifications that the software will do, this is how fast it will operate. These are all the various aspects of it. And it completely meets those specifications. If it doesn't meet spec, we'll give you your money back. But it absolutely meets specification."

One day we woke up as a company and realized one of the hardest things—that we couldn't keep acting like this entrepreneurial start-up, pushing rules and breaking them. We had to change everything about how we looked at the world. We also needed to change how we measured our success—from building great products and shipping them to measuring our success based on our customers' success. That meant that when we were successful, they got what they wanted.

■ Customers—A Huge Transformation

For an engineering-oriented company like Trilogy, this was not easy. Our people felt, "We can't tie ourselves to our customers, we just need to build great products. Customer success will never be a value at Trilogy, ever."

It was a huge transformation.

One of my developers walked into my office after we started this and said, "Joe, I just don't want to do this. I want to shut my door, and I just want to code—and I want to build great products that get awards. If I have to go worry what the customers care about, I just don't want to do it."

But we believed in our heart that this was what we had to do. We had to make the transformation—and get out of that old mindset.

So that developer left.

We decided to measure this new method by actually asking our customers. Every six months, we call up the senior business owner for our customer and we say, "You had some reason you bought this thing, some reason why you wanted it, or some business benefit you wanted. Have you got it yet? Yes or no? Are you guys successful?"

And then we'd measure it. When we first started this program, the first time we called all our customers, only 7 percent said yes. We didn't even know who to call sometimes.

We've been working on the program and are now up above 80 percent of our customers saying they've gotten their return on the system. But the mindset and the change around those standards of what you hold yourself accountable to are very hard to understand, very hard to deal with—because it's not in your control in a lot of cases. When you have a spec and you can meet it, it's very tangible. When you ask somebody, "Are you successful," it's very different.

Over the course of the last year—with all the things that are happening in the marketplace—we have come to a new understanding that has put us in a good place for the times.

What you really want from the people you do business with—and the people you work with—is that you want to feel that they are thinking in your terms, holding themselves to the highest standard.

■ **"Just Tell Me It's Going to Work"**

I realized why our success with our customers was actually having such a powerful impact. For most companies, when they
look at the enterprise software world, it's one of the largest capital expenditures they make outside their domain of expertise.
When Boeing builds a new airplane, it allocates a billion dollars
for the development of the next generation. The current president ran the 777, he knows everything about it. He's a domain
expert. But when he allocates hundreds of millions of dollars for
his big ERP systems project, he doesn't feel comfortable, didn't
know anything substantive about it. What he wanted to do was
look everybody in the eye and say, "Just tell me it's going to
work." And there's nothing beyond that besides the brand, the
person. Can they deliver?

This whole issue is so important. When I teach our Trilogy
University classes, a lot of these new college graduates look at
me and say, "Joe, we're not like the crooks down at Enron." Or,
"We wouldn't cheat like the guys at WorldCom. It's just not a
big issue, let's not worry about it."

That can't be more wrong. Because the basis of everything
we do today is trust and integrity. The whole system works on
this—and if it's not there, everything else crumbles. It doesn't
matter if you have the greatest product in the world if the people don't trust you! If you can't trust the other side—if you don't
believe that they're full of integrity—then it's over.

And what used to just be words for most people, because of
what's gone on in the last year, is now center stage. It should be.

Everybody in the business world has to turn this negative
image around, we'll have to become pillars.

I know friends who worked at Enron, and you ask, "How
could they let it happen?" One of them actually first got into a
dot-com, but it didn't work out. So he joined Enron—a "real
company" with "stability."

■ Another Enron Moment . . .

So the guy went to work at Enron. I was talking to him a few months into his new job. "I just got employee of the month, and they gave me a pin," he said. He was very proud. The guy was working in energy services, where they sold the energy contracts to big Fortune 500 companies. He'd found one contract where the accounting was wrong and an extra $25 million could be recognized, because they'd made a mistake.

A few months later, he wasn't so happy. "They took my pin away." It turns out he was reviewing another contract and found another mistake: $40 million that was too positive—and they had to back it out. He reported that up the ladder and it was all getting shut down. But he was pressing on. And his boss was pushing him, "Be quiet." The guy has since left Enron.

What would you do in that situation?

In his case, it wasn't, "I've got to fight it." He just left.

What would I do in that situation? I know what I want to say I'd do. I know what I'd like to do. I certainly hope that I would have pushed back hard—and not just have left Enron.

We need people who will push, who will be the pillars. When we changed our whole company to emphasize customer success, what we said was, "We're going to put everybody's bonus on whether the customer says yes or no." So when we call the customer, and say, "Are you successful—yes or no," if the answer's "no," the team doesn't get a bonus. And customers love that. They think that's the greatest thing in the world, because they're in control.

■ Waiting on Pins and Needles

You have to understand how we do these calls. We actually have the whole team, usually in another room, set for a big celebration. We celebrate if it's a "yes." So they're all waiting as the call's going on, champagne half-poured.

In one case, where client executives disagreed on how we had done, we did not give the bonus. We sat up and said to the team, "This is not what we're all about. What we are all about is being aligned with the customer—it's not about whether we're able to hit the letter of the law, ignoring the spirit of the law."

That's very much like when we used to tell our customers, "Our product hits spec; it's too bad you couldn't get it to work, but the contract is completely valid. We're not breaking it."

We said, "What we're trying to do is move beyond that, from what the letter of the law says into what the customer really wants."

So we have to move our standards to a higher level. It's taken us a long time to get there—a lot of pain and agony, because it costs you something. In this case, it cost the team their bonus.

Over the last two years, we've had to turn down somewhere between $30 million and $50 million worth of business that we didn't think we could deliver successfully. When we sat down with the customer—and they wanted to buy it—we said, "We can't commit to that, we won't sell this deal."

When you're sitting there—faced with laying off your friends because you're not getting the contract—and you have to decide whether you can make it work, those are really tough decisions. But they're critical ones if we're going to get this baby back on track and restore confidence. Every single person must be accountable to a much higher—dramatically higher—standard.

You're faced with judgment calls every day. And what you want to know is that the people you're working with—your teammates—and you are all thinking on the same page.

So, as you go through this process, a lot of old standards change. It is a different world.

When I first describe how we got funded, how we started Trilogy, most young people say, "Wow—that's really cool." They take it as some great example of high-tech entrepreneurship. But I couldn't start my company today the way I did a decade ago. Times are different. What was acceptable and right—even the lore of start-ups, the cool stuff of pushing the boundaries, breaking the rules a little bit is not acceptable in today's world.

It is a different world. And we all have to move toward a higher standard to serve it.

Exercises in Ethics

Joe Liemandt's great awakening came when he moved Trilogy from a product-function entrepreneurial focus to a company providing products and services that contribute to customers' success.

In Liemandt's case, this meant moving:

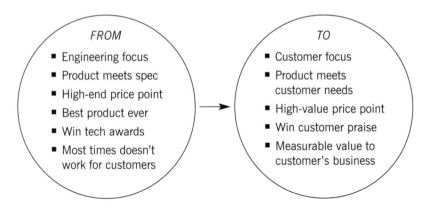

FROM	TO
▪ Engineering focus	▪ Customer focus
▪ Product meets spec	▪ Product meets customer needs
▪ High-end price point	▪ High-value price point
▪ Best product ever	▪ Win customer praise
▪ Win tech awards	▪ Measurable value to customer's business
▪ Most times doesn't work for customers	

1. What would a similar transformational leap be for your business?

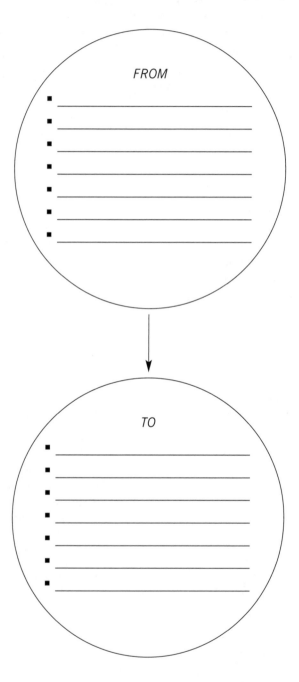

2. How could making a change to the new focus enhance the following for your business?

   a. Customer loyalty:

   _____

   _____

   _____

   _____

   _____

   _____

   _____

   _____

   _____

   b. Perception as ethical company:

   _____

   _____

   _____

   _____

   _____

   _____

   _____

3. How would you, like Liemandt, alter your reward system to best serve the new business focus?

   _____

   _____

   _____

   _____

   _____

   _____

   _____

   _____

4. How would making such a change alter your Teachable Point of View on business ethics with regard to:

a. Your business:

_____

_____

_____

_____

_____

_____

_____

_____

b. Your commitment to business ethics:

_____

_____

_____

_____

_____

_____

_____

_____

c. Matching employee rewards and performance:

_____

_____

_____

_____

_____

_____

_____

_____

13

Ethics, Virtuousness, and Constant Change

Kim Cameron
*Professor of Organizational Behavior
and Human Resource Management
University of Michigan Business School*

Editors' Note: Emerging research on virtuousness, or behaving humanely, can have a powerful, remarkably positive and reproductive effect on individuals as well as the organizations they populate. This virtuousness and all that it brings to an organization can provide fixed points in seas of uncertainty, reliable anchors to help leaders navigate the constant change with some stable principles to guide them. That stability of core principles also makes for more successful people and organizations, especially in the turbulent world in which we all live today.

It's not news that we live in a dynamic, turbulent, even chaotic world.

Almost no one would try to predict with any degree of certainty what the world will be like in ten years. Things change too fast. We know that the technology currently exists, for example, to put the equivalent of a full-size computer in a wristwatch, or inject the equivalent of a laptop computer into a person's bloodstream. New computers will probably be etched on molecules instead of silicon wafers. The mapping of the human genome is probably the greatest source for change, for not only can we now change a banana into an agent to inoculate people against malaria but new organ development and physiological regulation promises to dramatically alter the lifestyles of whole populations.

Who can predict the changes that will result? Thus, not only is change currently ubiquitous and constant but almost everyone predicts that it will escalate exponentially.

The trouble is, when everything is changing, it is impossible to manage change. Let me explain: Let's say you're flying an airplane, moving through space. Everything is changing. You're constantly moving. The trouble is, it is impossible to guide the plane unless you can find a fixed point, something that doesn't change. You cannot control the plane if everything is moving. Consider the last flight of John Kennedy Jr., for example. He began to fly at dusk up the New England coast, losing sight of land. In the gathering dark, he lost sight of the horizon line as well. He lost his fixed point. The result was disorientation, and he flew his plane into the ocean, probably without knowing he was headed toward water. He couldn't manage change without a stable referent—something that didn't change.

■ With Instability, People Change Rules

When nothing is stable—when they have no fixed points, dependable principles, or stable benchmarks—people tend to make up their own rules. They make sense of the ambiguity and chaos they experience by deciding for themselves what is real and what is appropriate.

Recently, it has become clear that in high-pressure, high-velocity environments, some people in the energy-trading, telecommunications, and accounting industries simply made up their own rules. They ended up cheating, or lying, or waffling not only because it was to their economic advantage but because they had created their own rationale for what was acceptable. Conditions were changing constantly, and they let their rules change with them.

This danger of constantly changing conditions illustrates why ethics, values, and principles are more important now than ever. They serve as fixed points. They determine what is right and wrong, appropriate and inappropriate, on a universal basis, every time.

Integrity simply means maintaining unfailing values and principles, following through, doing what you say, being consistent, reinforcing a fixed point. And the effects of integrity are obvious. Integrity allows people to trust in something, and to make sense of the situation even in ambiguous, turbulent, chaotic environments. It provides the basis upon which everything from the stock market to family relationships can continue to function successfully. Integrity makes management possible under conditions of change.

■ En Route to Virtuousness

But something else is also crucial for success in human relationships and in organizations during turbulent times. Integrity—living consistent ethical principles—represents only one of two conditions that must be present. Let me explain the second condition by using a continuum like the one shown in Figure 13.1.

Think first of the human body. The large majority of medical research, and almost all of a physician's time, is spent trying to get people from the left point on the physiological continuum (illness) to the middle (health). This middle point represents an absence of illness or injury. Very little is known about how to get people from the middle point to the state of wellness on the right.

Psychologically the same thing occurs. More than 95 percent of psychological research in the last fifty years has focused on closing the gap between the left point and the middle point—overcoming depression, anxiety, stress, or emotional difficulties. Little is known about how to get people from a condition of health to a state of flourishing vitality, or what's referred to as "flow" in psychology.

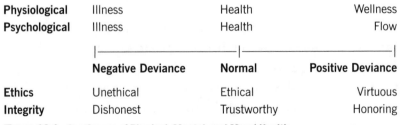

	Negative Deviance	Normal	Positive Deviance
Physiological	Illness	Health	Wellness
Psychological	Illness	Health	Flow
Ethics	Unethical	Ethical	Virtuous
Integrity	Dishonest	Trustworthy	Honoring

Figure 13.1. Continuum of Physical, Mental, and Moral Health.

Most of what we know about human physiology and psychology is how to overcome weakness or illness and reach a state of normality.

Now look at ethics and integrity on the continuum. Unethical behavior is that which produces harm. It violates principles. It does damage. We spend a lot of time—in our writing about ethics, in our legislation, in the popular press—addressing unethical behavior. The large majority of our attention is spent reminding leaders and organizations to behave ethically, honestly, with integrity. That usually means an absence of harm—behaving consistently, being trustworthy, not damaging others or the system.

Hardly any attention is given, however, to the right side of the continuum. I refer to that side as representing *virtuousness*. It is not only a condition of not producing harm, it is a condition of doing good, honoring others, taking a positive stance—of behaving in ways where self-interest is not the driving motivation.

■ The Relevance of Virtuousness

Unfortunately, words such as *virtuousness* and *honor* are often relegated to Sunday School, philosophy, or right-wing fanaticism. Their application in the world of work is viewed with skepticism or disdain. Managers frequently say: "These concepts are simply not relevant to me and to my company. We're in a competitive battleground. Virtuousness may be fine as a discussion topic at church or at a late-night coffee bar, but it's too soft and fuzzy to be relevant to the world of stock price pressures, competitive positioning, and customer complaints."

On the other hand, here comes the crucial point. We have recently begun a series of studies in which we measured the virtuousness of various kinds of organizations, mainly business organizations. We measured virtues such as compassion, integrity, forgiveness, trust, and optimism—factors usually included on lists of universally valued virtues.

We discovered that organizations with high scores on virtuousness significantly outperform organizations with low scores on virtuousness. We measured performance using factors such as profitability, productivity, innovation, quality, customer retention, and employee loyalty. More virtuous firms made more money than less virtuous firms. Virtuous firms recovered from downsizing and retained customers and employees more effectively than nonvirtuous firms did. Virtuous firms were more creative and innovative than nonvirtuous firms.

The implication is straightforward: not only must individuals and organizations avoid doing harm—that is, they must behave ethically—they must also act virtuously. Virtuousness is associated with positive outcomes, not just the absence of negative outcomes. It produces positive energy in systems, enables growth and vitality in people, and enhances the probability of extraordinarily positive performance. Virtuousness pays dividends. Doing good helps organizations do well.

■ Providing That "Fixed Point"

In conditions of turbulent change, virtuousness also serves both as a fixed point, a benchmark for making sense of ambiguity, and as a source of resilience, protecting the system against harm.*

The reason virtuousness has this kind of impact is because of two attributes. Virtuousness produces an amplifying effect, and virtuousness also produces a buffering effect.

---

*For details regarding the empirical studies described in this section, please get in touch with the author at cameronk@umich.edu.

Amplification

By *amplifying* I mean that virtuousness is self-perpetuating. When people are exposed to virtuous acts, they are attracted to them. They are elevated by them. They tend to reproduce them. When we observe virtuousness, we are inspired by it. This is similar to something called the *phototropic effect*. If you put a plant in the window, over time it will lean toward the light. All living systems—including human physiological, psychological, emotional, and intellectual systems—are subject to the same phenomenon. They have a tendency toward the positive and away from the negative. Virtuousness has that same attractive quality, and it tends to produce self-perpetuating positive effects.

Recent research has found, for example, that individuals who are full of gratitude tend to be healthier than those who feel victimized. The same goes for people whose lives are characterized by forgiveness, compassion, integrity, and other virtues. They are healthier both physiologically and emotionally.

For example, if you give out flu shots and measure the number of antibodies in the recipients' systems twenty-four hours later, the virtuous people will have more antibodies— they are healthier—than the others. People who are optimistic and positive actually heal faster and more completely from illness and injuries than pessimists do. People demonstrating more virtuousness learn faster, remember longer, and do better in mental functioning tests than others. Human systems tend to respond positively to virtuousness and goodness.

Just as these dynamics occur in individuals, similar dynamics also occur in organizations. Organizational performance tends to improve when virtuousness is fostered and nurtured. When people see others behaving humanely, they tend to behave humanely as well.

Integrity, compassion, and trust, for example, create an environment where people are encouraged to be their best, where innovativeness, loyalty, and quality are likely to be higher. That's the virtuous cycle. The amplifying nature of virtuousness causes it to reproduce itself and to improve organizational performance over time.

Buffering

The second reason virtuousness has this effect is its *buffering* attribute. That is, virtuousness helps inoculate the organization against harm in the face of trauma. It is now well established, for example, that downsizing leads to deteriorating performance in most organizations. This occurs, at least partly, because people are hurt or offended, relationships are destroyed, trust is battered, psychological contracts are broken, organizational memory is lost, secrecy escalates, and the threat-rigidity response occurs (threatened people and threatened organizations become rigid).

These findings have been confirmed over and over again. We found in our research, however, that virtuous organizations do not suffer the same debilitating and deteriorating effects of downsizing. They also bounce back quicker from any downturns. Less virtuous organizations are less resilient.

This is similar to what happens with individuals. Virtuous people who get cancer, become quadriplegics, or suffer life-altering harm tend to be more resilient than others. They bounce back sooner and experience more happiness and more fulfillment in their lives than others do. Life satisfaction scores measured before and after people become quadriplegics, for example, show this tendency. If people were optimistic, happy, and grateful before the loss of their limbs, they tend to be the same after. They bounce back sooner and relatively quickly reach the same emotional point where they were before. If they were depressed and sad, victimized, and vindictive before, they tend to be the same afterward. The trauma of the event doesn't cause life to change so much as the attributes the individual demonstrated beforehand.

It shouldn't come as a surprise, therefore, that the hallmark of great leaders in the twenty-first century—a century characterized above all by change and turbulence—is that they demonstrate not only ethical behavior—the absence of harm—but also virtuousness, producing active goodness.

Ethics and virtues serve as fixed points in a sea of confusion. They enable self-reinforcing positive outcomes to occur, and they buffer individuals and organizations from the verities of a world in which harm, damage, violations of principles, selfishness, and greed are likely to be ubiquitous.

Exercises in Ethics

Virtuousness encompasses compassion, humility, forgiveness, gratitude, integrity, optimism and similar dimensions—things that can serve as buffers to keep your business from collapsing in a storm (not unlike the scenario you created at the end of Chapter Ten).

1. List the fixed and stable points of ethics and integrity—the predictable, dependable, absolute tenets of your business—that will remain stable and assured no matter what ambiguity, change, or chaos hits your company.

_____

_____

_____

_____

_____

_____

_____

2. Building on the fixed points you just identified, describe the perception of virtuousness in your company that you would like your constituents to hold.

_____

_____

_____

☐

_____

_____

_____

_____

3. What changes, if any, does your company need to make to achieve this perception of virtuousness?

_____

_____

_____

_____

_____

_____

4. How would you describe the value of this virtuousness—and its "buffering effect"—in adding it to your Teachable Point of View on business ethics?

_____

_____

_____

_____

_____

_____

_____

_____

_____

_____

_____

_____

14

The Best Ethical Choices Come When Long-Term Impact Rules

Tim Fort
Associate Professor of Business Ethics
University of Michigan Business School

Editors' Note: How a company behaves in a pinch usually comes down to its core ethics. These often reflect choices that leaders made many years before. By openly discussing the challenges an organization faces and the values it stands for, ethics get cemented into the culture of the organization to drive behavior when it counts. A company like Johnson & Johnson works at its ethics—and it paid off. Ditto for H.B. Fuller. Both saved their reputations when put to the test. At Arthur Andersen and Enron, the cultures were not ingrained with the strong ethics to stop or say no, and they paid the price. The most important thing a company can do is determine—and then regularly discuss—its values and ethics.

Public attention to business ethics ebbs and flows. In the 1970s, following ITT's bribing of foreign officials, one of the results was passage of the Foreign Corrupt Practices Act—a legal response. In the late 1980s and early 1990s, the sale of junk bonds under questionable circumstances was met with restrictions making that less likely—a regulatory response.

Today we're looking at misleading and false financial statements, excessive executive profits from stock sales, and the like, and wondering whether Enron will change everything.

As before, this attention will change things for a time, but five or ten years from now, we'll see some other kind of misbehavior that we'll become very upset about and we'll shake our heads. But trying to learn from past mistakes may put us in a better position for the next go-around—which, hopefully, won't be so bad.

Recently, we've certainly seen a number of bad apple examples, such as WorldCom and Enron, that make us mad. But there's one case that just makes me sad—the Arthur Andersen case. It makes me sad because Arthur Andersen was founded by the Arthur Andersen, a man who staked his company's reputation—his own reputation—on the willingness to say no to rich organizations that wanted him to falsify their accounting documents.

Andersen said, "No. We'll find other ways to make our money. We're not going to have our reputation be sullied."

In subsequent years, Arthur Andersen was a leader in promoting business ethics. The firm ran a wonderful program in the Chicago area training people to teach business ethics in business schools, and it funded some of the best research on what makes ethical programs work, or not, in multinational corporations. To see what has befallen Arthur Andersen—and to see that name disparaged—is a truly sad sidelight to these scandals. It also underscores the importance of sustaining the momentum of what's important to an organization—so that, in a measure that could have saved Arthur Andersen, business ethics is not merely a series of wonderful programs for outsiders but a way of life inside the company.

■ A Pattern of Transgressions

Companies, like people, aren't perfect. They make mistakes. If this had been a single action with Andersen and Enron, people would have been upset, but the companies probably would have survived. Instead, it was a series of repeated transgressions that took down Enron and eroded Andersen's reputation.

Federal Reserve Chairman Alan Greenspan appeared before Congress in 2002, saying that in marketing services, as opposed to manufactured products, your reputation is your stock and trade. If you are an oil trader, as opposed to an oil producer, or if you are an accounting firm, what you are producing is largely related to your trustworthiness. If you do something to undermine that, then you very well may not have a company anymore. The 2002 corporate scandals were a great example of that.

One company that did build up a reputational safety net to withstand a tough situation was the H.B. Fuller Co., located in the Twin Cities. Fuller had a longtime reputation for being a socially responsible company—doing really good work with its employees, the community, a very interesting and admirable company. It ran into a problem about ten years ago with kids' sniffing glue from a product the company manufactured in Central America, particularly Honduras and Guatemala.

Fuller announced that it was going to get out of that market segment completely—then turned around and didn't do it. Fuller tried to say it really had promised only to reformulate the product, or to sell it in certain kinds of distribution formats, but there was clear evidence that it had, in fact, promised to get out. *Dateline NBC* exposed the fact that Fuller had stayed in the questionable segment of the glue business. Ultimately, after another seven years, the company finally did get out, but it was only after its reputation had taken a significant beating. But it did come through the troubles—because, with all of Fuller's history of good corporate citizenship, the glue case was seen as more of an aberration than example of the company's norm.

One thing that helped Fuller recover is that the glue it was manufacturing—used to glue shoes together—was a business-to-business product, not a direct-to-consumer product. So Fuller had insulation that could make it easier to salvage its reputation.

Andersen's actions, in contrast, were prominent and repeated. The story was easily captured in headlines, and anybody who could balance a checkbook could understand. Even though people might not understand all the various accounting technicalities, they could understand basic notions of balancing books and when things really are or aren't on the books. They could tell something was wrong—and that was devastating to Andersen.

Unfortunately, Andersen's demise hurt a lot of good people, too. Many reputations were damaged, even though only a few people in Andersen did unethical things. Now many people are living under a cloud even though they were good people who did nothing wrong.

■ Knowing When to Stay or Leave

Sometimes people struggle to search for a perfect ethical answer. One of the key wisdoms to learn is when it's best to get out of a situation and when to make a bad situation better by staying involved.

I did tax returns for a big client for a few years. The CEO came in one day and said, "I'm paying too much in taxes." I proposed some aggressive strategies that we could consider. He said, "Make up some deductions."

"What do you mean, make up some deductions?" I responded. "What are they?"

He said, "They're not there; just make them up."

I explained that we couldn't do that.

He said, "Well, then you can't be my lawyer."

I gave him his papers—and he walked out.

Sometimes the only real ethical answer is to leave—which is what Arthur Andersen, the man, did.

H.B. Fuller initially started to follow this route, but then it decided to stay and actually do some things to make the situation better. They looked at reformulation of the glue and changing the distribution channels to not sell small cans of glue that kids could get and sniff. These were not perfect answers, but they did help.

As Frederick Bird writes in *The Muteness of Managers*, people actually know an awful lot about ethical values. They were raised in homes where ethics were talked about or thought about. But the presumption is that once you walk into the workplace, those things fall away—and you talk about business. One reason managers are reluctant to bring up ethical issues is that they are viewed as "soft." And if you're going to get ahead in business, everybody knows you have to be tough and hard-headed—not soft and hung up on ethics.

I've always found that view to be curious because two of my moral heroes were Jesus and Gandhi—and both got killed for their beliefs. That doesn't seem very "soft" to me.

■ Our Reluctance to Talk About Ethics

Still, people are reluctant to talk about ethical values—and if you don't talk about ethical values, you can't, with confidence, expect to have ethical decisions in your organization. You won't get enough practice at making and reviewing the ethical decisions.

Aristotle said most ethical actions are things we don't even think about, because they're such a regular part of our life that they become natural. By eliminating discussion about ethics in the workplace, you end up with dilemmas—where there are no clear answers. One way to minimize such dilemmas is similar to the way that you instill quality in the workplace—to regularly talk about standards and have people point out defects in the processes. To make ethics sustainable, you must make it a regular part of the corporate conversation—with people actually raising the issues. That takes guts. But there's no other way it's going to happen. You can have all the policies in the world, all the plans, wonderful codes of conduct, but it still takes human beings to say, "I think this is important."

In privately held companies, it may be easier to come to agreement on what the most critical ethical interests might be, whereas, in a public company with 5 million shareholders, many contend the only common denominator may be making money. Yet there is something in between, represented by companies such as Johnson & Johnson, Timberland, or the *New York Times,* which have clear public statements of what they stand for. Such companies have been more successful in maintaining the integration of ethical values in their business. These values can be sustained by how the organizations make decisions and the cultures they create.

■ The Critical Questions on Ethics

To have ethical decisions, you need an agreed-upon process to consider what is happening. The process doesn't have to be very complicated—this simple six-part moral decision-making framework proposed by my predecessor at Michigan, LaRue Hosmer, will serve you well:

- What's the moral issue?
- Who has been harmed?
- In what ways?
- What are the alternatives that exist?
- What facts need to be known to make a reasoned decision?
- What are the personal impacts on the person making the decision?

Without such an established format to work through, research shows most people are predisposed to value their own self-interest over the interest of others, defaulting to what seems "good for me now." But what may be missed is "What's good for me in the long term," because you may not have adequately considered the impact on your reputation and its effect down the road.

This framework is not the only one. The right answer can come from any kind of formalized process, so long as it lays out what the facts are, what the different alternatives might be, and then asks: What is the obligation to the shareholders? What's the obligation to other important stakeholders such as employees or customers? Simply asking simple questions like that can significantly broaden discussions of what you do, or should do.

If Enron had asked seriously about its responsibility to shareholders, its crisis might have been avoided. If its executives had asked about their responsibility to employees, they might have never so aggressively pitched their stock while dumping it. Honestly looking at its three main stakeholder groups—shareholders, customers, and employees—would tell Enron a lot about the impact of trading energy futures to gain excess profits at the expense of customers, for instance. Is this or that fair treatment of those three key constituent groups?

Simply posing these questions goes a long way to making a decision that's balanced, that would protect your reputation.

In addition, creating corporate cultures that reinforce the values that you want people to live by is essential. You can rely on people's personal honesty and integrity to an extent, but you ultimately need a culture that supports those behaviors and that doesn't punish people for taking an action you want them to take. Without that support, employees will only do what's right so many times—and then they're either going to leave, or they're going to give up and cave in to whatever behaviors are being rewarded.

Enron stressed pushing the limits and had a corporate culture to push everything. The chief financial officer had a cube on his desk that said, "When Enron says it's going to rip your face off, it will rip your face off." That's the same guy who set up the partnerships with himself as the general partner—and then told people, "I'm going to be able to do better than anybody else because I have inside information." Simply a blatant disregard for the law. He did it on videotape, no less.

■ Pushing the Limits—Too, Too Far

Pushing the limits can be good—pushing your personal capabilities, for instance, can lead to things you never thought you could do. But if you systematically set up a culture where you're trying to violate the law or get around it, that's hardly ethical. I had two kinds of clients when I practiced law. One said, "This is my business, and I want to make sure that what I'm doing is legal." The other said, "Here is my business. Tell me what the law is—and tell me how to get around the law." Those are very different attitudes.

You can have similar debates about how far an ethical business should go. There's one notion of making sure you obey the law. But studies have shown that if your corporate goal is only to obey the law, you'll never inspire people enough to even get into compliance with the law. People don't go home at night happy that they resisted the temptation to not comply with an anti-trust law. They don't brag, "Gee honey, guess what I did today. I complied with anti-trust laws, and I'm proud of it." It just doesn't move you.

Take the Johnson & Johnson culture as another example. In 1982, I was a third-year law student at Northwestern. Whenever I felt under the weather, my medication of choice was Extra-Strength Tylenol. I wasn't feeling very good one fall afternoon and was out of Extra-Strength Tylenol capsules. So I decided to go across the street to the local Walgreen's in the Old Town area of Chicago and buy some. Just as I was walking out the door, my roommate said, "Wait a minute, I think I've got some in my medicine cabinet." He did. So I didn't go across the street. An unfortunate flight attendant, however, did go across that street that same afternoon, to buy Extra-Strength Tylenol capsules; she took them—and died from cyanide poisoning. It was the classic and tragic Johnson & Johnson cyanide poisoning case, which struck very close to home for me.

As is well known, Johnson & Johnson, within the week, yanked every bottle of Extra-Strength Tylenol capsules off the shelves across the country.

Why?

In a world when many companies may seek compliance with the law, just to avoid impropriety, Johnson & Johnson said that the first thing it stood for was to provide safe products to the mothers, fathers, patients, doctors, and nurses who use them. After that Johnson & Johnson would talk about obligations to employees, suppliers, and—when all is said and done, at the very end—its famous Credo says that if we respect all these people, our shareholders will receive a fair return on their investment.

"We couldn't meet our aspiration, our goal of making sure we had safe products," Johnson & Johnson said. "We had to take them off the market." And people at Johnson & Johnson will tell you now, twenty years later, that this is real stuff, that the corporate Credo is serious, and not just some statement from 1982.

In 2002, Johnson & Johnson ran a program in Brazil where it feeds its workers. It's just a snack, but the workers eat every day. You can argue that a fed worker is going to be more productive than a starving one, so it's just good business. That's the point! When you look at the needs of people you work with, it's not something you have to do. But what Johnson & Johnson seeks is to achieve a good. When you're seeking to achieve a good like that, other things start to fall into place.

That's a very different corporate culture from one that either flouts the law or just seeks to stay out of trouble. This is an aspirational approach, which leads to regular discussion of ethical values and virtues. Now, Johnson & Johnson isn't perfect. It gets sued. It makes mistakes. But, at the same time, its people have a better chance of resisting the temptation that exists everywhere than people do in a company with a corporate culture more like Enron's.

In the end, there are ethical choices that every company makes about what kind of a company it wants to be. And, in the long run, those choices make all the difference in the world.

Exercises in Ethics

1. Picture making ethics and integrity in business what Tim Fort calls "a regular part of the corporate conversation":

   a. What specific topics and examples would you include?

   _____

   _____

   _____

   _____

   _____

   _____

   _____

   b. What vulnerabilities could you face in making these issues part of the conversation?

   _____

   _____

   _____

   _____

   _____

   _____

   _____

2. Use the ethical decision-making framework described by Fort to expand beyond a self-interest focus to fully examine your alternatives on the most controversial ethical issue you listed here—making that discussion part of the "corporate conversation," as well.

   a. What is the moral or ethical issue?

   _____

   _____

   _____

   _____

   _____

b. Who has been harmed?

_____

_____

_____

_____

_____

_____

_____

c. In what ways?

_____

_____

_____

_____

_____

_____

_____

d. What alternatives exist?

_____

_____

_____

_____

_____

_____

_____

e. What facts are needed to make a rational decision?

_____

_____

_____

_____

_____

_____

_____

f. What is the personal impact on you as the decision maker?

_____

_____

_____

_____

_____

_____

_____

g. What is the impact on other stakeholders?

_____

_____

_____

_____

_____

_____

h. What would corporate consensus, based on the conversations and discussions, say was the best alternative response that came up?

_____

_____

_____

_____

_____

_____

i. What do you think is the best response for you as the leader to take?

_____

_____

_____

_____

_____

_____

☐

j. If the corporate consensus and your own answer are different, how will you reconcile and explain that difference?

_____

_____

_____

_____

_____

_____

_____

3. How would you incorporate these choices and dilemmas into your Teachable Point of View on business ethics?

_____

_____

_____

_____

_____

_____

_____

_____

_____

_____

_____

_____

_____

_____

_____

_____

_____

_____

_____

_____

PART 3

The Ethical Future

Ultimately, the commitment to high ethics and the related reinforcement experiences that the next generation of business leaders bring to their tasks will have a mighty influence on the integrity of their business practices.

This part begins with a glimpse into the experiences of some such future leaders by looking at ethical dilemmas that incoming students in the University of Michigan Business School Class of 2004 have already faced in their business careers. The chapter also underscores these students' learnings—and the impact those ethical experiences have had in shaping the students' ethical underpinnings.

The following two chapters—by Professor LaBrent Chrite and by Eleanor Josaitis, founder of Focus: HOPE—explore two areas where a company's ethical commitments in society will take on greater reality in the future. The first is in business expansion into developing countries, especially those with open and transparent capital markets—with public-private partnering for success—and the integrity with which a company operates in these emerging markets. The second is in the citizenship commitments a business organization and its leaders make to the communities where they do business, highlighting Focus: HOPE as a model of inner-city human development.

This part and this book conclude with a focus on the importance of leaders developing their own Teachable Point of View on business ethics to use in teaching their people and in developing Virtuous Teaching Cycles throughout their organizations. The book also concludes with a final Exercise in Ethics that helps readers pull together all their previous exercises to craft and launch their ethics teaching.

15

Students Meet Ethical Dilemmas in Their Workplace Challenges

Noel M. Tichy and Six MBA Students
University of Michigan Business School

Editors' Note: While ethical failures at the top of companies such as Enron, WorldCom, Tyco, and ImClone produced spectacular headlines and sent prosecutors, regulators, and lawmakers scrambling for responses, senior-level moral blowouts such as these are rare. Far more common—and potentially far more costly to individual companies and to the economy as a whole—are the ethical dilemmas faced every day by the individuals who work within organizations. The decisions and actions of the people who design the products, deliver the services, interact with the customers, and write the reports are critical to maintaining an organization's integrity and trust between buyers and sellers, lenders and borrowers, employers and employees.

We asked incoming MBA students in the University of Michigan Business School class of 2004 to talk about issues they had personally experienced on the job and the inherent ethical dilemmas they had faced. The responses from these young professionals—ranging from twenty-one to forty-three years of age with one to eighteen years of work experience—amply demonstrate that workers at all levels routinely must make moral decisions that affect their companies, their clients, their careers, and ultimately the free-market society.

Their responses range from courageous to pragmatic. Sometimes the students reported that they hung tough and stood by their morals. But sometimes they gave in to the less ethical forces in their environment. In almost all cases, when asked to reflect on the events and develop a Teachable Point of View, they concluded that selling out your morals is never a good idea. Over the next two years, while they are students at Michigan, their professors' job is to help them put their TPOVs into action—and to teach others, as well.

■ Student #1: Adjusting the Report

The Armed Services prides itself on being a values-based organization. It passes out laminated cards detailing the Armed Services core values to all soldiers, requiring them to wear the card around their necks. However, such dedication to values often falls short in practice, especially in situations where a zero-defect mentality is applied. Some specific reports can have very significant ramifications on a leader's career. There is often very little margin for error. It is in preparing these reports that I personally faced the greatest ethical dilemmas of my career.

There is one monthly report that all war-fighting units prepare. It is compiled at each level of the organization and forwarded to the Armed Services at the Pentagon. These reports detail war-fighting capabilities from the viewpoint of personnel and equipment readiness. Each leader is evaluated on the ability to maintain a high readiness rating. Thus, inherent in the system is the pressure for leaders to manipulate the statistical viewpoint to support their careers.

This report is a snapshot view of an organization taken on the sixteenth of every month. It details who is *deployable*—available to go to war—broken down by job title and rank. It also describes the reasons why individuals are nondeployable, whether for injury, disciplinary action, pregnancy, or because of current deployment.

Leaders are under tremendous pressure to ensure that they appear ready for war, since that is their organization's primary purpose. This results in the temptation to adjust their snapshot to present an appearance of readiness, even if that condition may not exactly exist. Because of the descriptive nature of many of the report's categories, a large gray area exists, leaving much room for interpretation. For example, say Sergeant Joe Collins has a sprained ankle and cannot run, he is officially nondeployable. However, in reality a sprained ankle would not stop him from deploying to war if his skills were badly needed. Additionally, his ankle might be healed by the eighteenth of the month.

Therefore, while the letter of the regulation governing the report requires that the guy be counted as nondeployable, common sense would list him as deployable. Additionally, when a job evaluation is based in large part upon this report, the temptation to distort facts becomes even stronger.

Every month in the Armed Services, leaders are faced with the dilemma of accurately portraying unit readiness at the potential expense of their career. Because this dilemma occurs at every level, it creates an organizational climate where values and ethics are preached, but not always put into practice.

On a personal level, as one who prepared the monthly report, I was put in the position of reporting what our readiness statistics actually were according to regulation. I was frequently instructed to manipulate the report to present a very different picture. I was never directly instructed to lie, but was told to omit specific facts that dramatically altered the image of our unit's readiness.

Therefore, I was forced to choose between disobeying a lawful, direct order and placing my signature on a report verifying facts that I knew to be incomplete. Both these options were unethical and illegal under military law and ethics.

Outcome

In two years in this position, I was able to partially resolve this dilemma. I became skilled in presenting the statistical breakdown to leaders who had little technical understanding of the subject. Furthermore, I learned that if I forced these leaders to state their positions clearly, they would inevitably make the ethical choice. The question, "Are you asking me to lie on this report?" guaranteed that they would back away from their original unethical decision. This solution was imperfect, at best, since it demonstrated my integrity at the expense of my loyalty. Since both integrity and loyalty are specified Armed Services values, I was only able to resolve one ethical dilemma by creating another.

TPOV

From this experience, I learned the danger of vocalizing a values system and then creating an organizational system that subverts it. By creating a zero-defect environment in an imperfect world, the Armed Services has put its leaders in a position where making the correct ethical decision ensures their careers will not be successful. It is clearly set up to ensure the advancement of unethical leaders.

I have often been told, "Bad news doesn't get better with time." While this statement is certainly true, breaking bad news to a boss is often a nerve-racking experience, since it forces you to choose between your personal gain and the organization's best interests. Many bosses have been known to adopt a "kill the messenger" mentality, so workers are tempted to hide or ignore information that is detrimental to the organization. This allows problems to fester and grow, becoming harder to fix and harder to bring to the boss's attention later. This self-perpetuating cycle can eventually cause the downfall of an organization by becoming an insolvable problem. Consistently and publically praising and rewarding employees who address bad news and problems can eliminate this problem. For this effort to be effective, however, it must permeate every level of an organization and be sponsored at the highest levels of leadership.

■ Student #2: Using Ideas Submitted by a Rejected Supplier

As a young project engineer, I was assigned the responsibility of automating the material handling of a plant and updating the stocking strategies in the warehouse of the same plant. This project was chosen by the company as part of a new approach in consulting suppliers. This new approach was to rebuild the relationship between our company and suppliers, to make them partners on each project. As a result of this new way of working with suppliers, there was a change in the request for quotation documents that we sent to the three selected suppliers on my project. Instead of writing the technical specifications of an automated handling system we had already designed, we sent suppliers the functional specifications regarding our throughput needs and also the description of the plant environment.

The three suppliers' answers were all different. Supplier A gave an answer that was simply out of scope not only for their solution but also for their price. Company B proposed a system that met our needs with minor insufficiencies, but the price they proposed was the lowest. Company C showed a thorough understanding of the problem and proposed a system that even took into account important concerns that we hadn't considered. Although C's solution was the most expensive, it was very effective.

The choice was between B and C. The purchasing department supported company B, while the best offer from my point of view was C. My boss also chose B and asked me to work with supplier B as a partner, to improve the system they had submitted so that their offer could become bearable. There started the dilemma!

I was committed to the success of the project, and I knew the automated system that C had designed was the best response to our needs. Thus, there was nothing more natural than undertaking the same solutions from C in the work with B. I couldn't help taking what I had seen in C's offer as a reference. On one hand, I felt it was unfair to C since they hadn't been kept as our partner on this project, yet we were about to use the ideas they had proposed.

I almost viewed this situation as a robbery. I remember that they trusted us when they gave us all their detailed studies and plans, while they were not required to do so. I was about to betray their trust. On the other hand, there was no violation of any law, even if we had signed an agreement mentioning that one supplier's offer could not be transmitted or showed to another supplier. Moreover, there was no legal intellectual property within C's ideas that I wanted to reuse.

Outcome

To find a way out of this dilemma, I looked for colleagues' advice. Most of them, including my boss, acknowledged the issues I was struggling with but pointed out the legal point of view and our company interest, which implied my interest. They said the business world was a jungle where everybody looked after their own interest without violating the laws, even if it was harmful to others. As I strongly wanted to make my project a success for the company and with the support from my colleagues and my boss, I just continued the easy way: applying company C's solutions to our project.

Since it was the first time my company used these functional specifications while consulting a supplier, I was asked to give feedback. Among the remarks I made was suggesting that we pay suppliers for making a bid with functional specifications. This suggestion was adopted for future projects and I felt better about my case, even if supplier C didn't benefit from this decision.

TPOV

Integrity is among the least common naturally shared values. It is a matter of finding the limit between the bearable and the unacceptable. Considering integrity, people won't draw the same conclusions if they aren't provided with the same vision. Nevertheless, people in the same company, the same business, or simply people who interact together need integrity as a shared value because it is the cornerstone of trust—and there is no community without trust. Business leaders should help build common limits, to make integrity become a shared value. One way is to ask yourself some simple questions when making decisions: Would I think it was fair if I were in the other person's shoes? Can I let people know what is going on without being concerned?

■ Student #3: Misrepresentations to a Client

In the late 1990s in Asia, ABC Consulting, a global consulting firm, was hired to implement several applications for a new major company. I was assigned to the Customer Care Department of the project. Because of the magnitude of the project, the client company requested that we bring in foreign experts who had a long trail of work experience in world-class telecom companies. However, we found it very difficult to find available foreign consultants within the time frame. So my company recruited several freelancers through a headhunting agency, and disguised them as our consultants from overseas offices.

I felt very uncomfortable with the situation. Cheap freelancers masquerading as expensive, top-notch consultants! I was one of the liars ripping off the client. In addition, as one of the few Asians in the project, I felt guilty for the Asian client members whom I often hung around with after work. I sometimes felt an impulse to let the cat out of the bag for the benefit of the Asian company, and moreover, for the prosperity of the Asian economy.

Outcome

I could not do anything to resolve this dilemma. I was just a junior consultant who had been with my firm about a year. I did not have the guts to tell the truth, betraying my colleagues and my company. I was more accustomed to maintaining peace and order in my nest. Though we were successful in deceiving the client, the project was not very successful. We had to worry about our Achilles' heel all the time, and the freelancers did not meet our expectations. Increasingly poor teamwork with them noticeably delayed the project schedule, disappointing the client. In the end, we failed to win the next phase project.

TPOV

Through this experience, I learned that a lack of business integrity leads to failure in the end. When you succeed in managing to escape a certain situation by yielding your integrity, you are just crossing a river—and you can never return. You will suffer from a guilty conscience—and will lose confidence in maintaining your relationship with your business partner. Your business will go down, as your partners lose trust in you. Therefore, if you are tempted to yield integrity to solve problems, do not forget that you could lose what reputation you have established in one moment by doing so.

■ Student #4: Offering Honest Assessments

During my career with an e-business consultancy, I spent several months developing a pure-play online banking strategy for a large regional bank. My client was interested in expanding its customer footprint by providing a host of financial services through a separately marketed national online bank. Working with its executive management team, I was charged with leading a market assessment to identify potential entry points into the online banking arena.

Prior to the engagement, I had recently completed a white paper regarding the key challenges facing the online banking industry. I understood that the online banking market was projected to experience tremendous growth in the following years;

however, many of the established online banks were having difficulty drawing customers and, more important, retaining them. Prohibitively high marketing costs, tight margins, and the convergence of online financial services created a highly competitive industry. Nevertheless, given the recent entry of competitors, my client was convinced that the development of an online bank presented an enormous revenue opportunity.

Reviewing the financials and demographic data for the competitive assessment confirmed many of my initial concerns. The pure-play online banking sector was saturated with competitors who had significantly greater financial resources and access to larger and more established customer bases. Even with a first-to-market advantage, these well-backed competitors were finding it difficult to retain customers and generate profits. Recognizing the poor prospects for success, I believed the client would be better served in exploring options in leveraging strengths in its established credit card business. However, my professional opinion introduced a dilemma.

In initial discussions regarding the scope of the project, the client had expressed the desire to complete the entire strategy development and subsequent implementation with our company. Completion of the project posed significant financial benefits for both our company and its shareholders. Because the client was determined to develop an online banking solution, recommending a change in that strategy meant potentially losing both the business and a tremendous revenue opportunity. Although I was aware of the potential financial cost of proposing an alternative solution, I decided that pursuing a course of action dictated by excessive client pressure and prospects for financial gain would undermine my professional obligation to provide my client with the best business solution. Additionally, advising the client to continue with a weak online banking strategy could damage the credibility of our company and compromise future client opportunities.

Outcome

After struggling with the dilemma between financial gain and professional obligation, I advised my client against entering the online banking market. I assembled several case studies to provide supporting evidence. I detailed competitor data, including financials and customer acquisition numbers, and outlined the key hurdles to entry. I also developed a presentation regarding the online credit card industry to provide ideas regarding alternatives to online banking that would allow the client to expand its nationwide customer reach. After considering my counsel, the client nonetheless decided to continue with a full online banking strategy development. They believed that by taking an approach where I could assist them in identifying and focusing on a niche customer segment, their potential outlook for success would be much better than that of their competitors.

Although recommending an alternative solution carried with it a potentially enormous financial opportunity cost, my candid counseling built confidence with the client, leading them not only to continue working with us on the strategy development but also to hire us for the follow-up implementation phase. With the downturn in the Internet industry and the failure of several Internet banks, they eventually decided to pull back from deploying the online banking solution and, instead, leveraged their card business to launch an Internet-only credit card—thereby validating my initial recommendation. If I had not recommended against the online banking strategy, our company would not only have lost any future business with my client, it would have lost credibility in the industry.

TPOV

I learned through this experience that while profits and short-term gains are often served by unethical and deceptive business practices, adhering to a higher ethical standard leads to stronger and longer-term business partnerships. It is relationships built on trust and honesty that generate lasting, sustainable business profitability.

Businesses operate efficiently on an underlying foundation of trust. Investors purchase securities because they trust the conviction of financial advisers and securities analysts just as companies seek strategic consulting advice to gain an honest assessment of the direction of their businesses. Without this basic level of business integrity, the entire business process collapses.

Although I discuss ethical business practices at a corporate level, it is at the individual level that business integrity and trust have the greatest impact. No matter how innovative or motivating a business leader, individuals cannot convincingly lead without a strong foundation of ethical values. This foundation forms the basis for developing trust with colleagues and building credibility with clients.

Leaders can have varying amounts of energy or innovation, but they cannot have varying levels of ethical values. The business process breaks down as soon as individuals become selective in applying business ethics. A perfect example of this situation is Martha Stewart's ImClone debacle. While her financial gain in the situation was minimal, questions concerning her business integrity have not only affected her own reputation but that of her company and ultimately her employees.

The failure of one individual to apply a standard level of business integrity has led to the downfall of many others. In recent years, developments such as accelerated stock option schedules have encouraged unethical business practices. With so much focus on short-term performance and financial gain, the business community has nurtured a dangerous environment. Business leaders and corporations must focus on developing individuals who foster core ethical business values, or we will continue to see massive breakdowns in the business process.

■ Student #5: Padding Projects to Inflate Client Costs

Sheila, my project manager, was the brightest star on the company's skyline. Newly acquired stock options tucked under her belt, she smiled at me appreciatively in acknowledgment of the fresh piece of code that I'd written. She was oblivious to the discomfort I was beginning to feel more strongly with every passing day. Why would she notice it, anyway? She had plenty to occupy her mind, including the fact that now that the project had been signed off, the sole responsibility for its successful execution was hers.

I, however, could not get over my knowledge that the code I was writing was not really essential or required for the application to run. The service we were providing to the customer for database system migration would have functioned effectively even without the business logic that our team was feverishly coding.

My discomfort started when she and the technical architect sidestepped my questions and doubts about the utility of my software module. My misgivings were further fortified when, in order to clear my own doubts, I dug out books and literature and was finally convinced about the real story. I was spending week after week writing software for a module that did not need to be included in the detailed design of the application in the first place. Instead, it was woven in cleverly during the design phase and was now carried over to the development phase of the project as an integral part of the application. The client would end up paying through the nose for this redundant work.

Outcome

I could not resolve the dilemma for several reasons:

- The project had already been signed off. My bringing up the issue at this stage would not change anything, and it would just be buried at a higher level. Maybe if this had come up during design, things would have been different. Since I wasn't a part of the design team, I wasn't aware of what exactly had happened then. So the timing was not right.

- There was no process in place for me to correct this immediately. I realized I could give my inputs through the reverse appraisal system six months later, but there was no process in place to do it now.

- I feared it would affect my career adversely. I admit having thought somewhat selfishly, though at the same time I vowed to myself to take up such issues when I reached the practice-unit leadership level in my career. I assume and hope to have more influence in preventing such things then. But at this stage, I couldn't figure out where to go for redress of this grievance without repercussions on my career.

TPOV

This incident helped draw my attention to the importance of ethics. It is a natural human trait to understand things best after having personally experienced them. It reinforced my belief in the importance of ethics in a business setting.

I struggled with the issue of who was wrong here. I couldn't really blame Sheila. It was the influence of the system. She was actually a victim of the prevailing culture that had developed in our practice unit ever since a new practice head had been appointed. He was ruthless about acquiring bigger and better projects at any cost. Integrity is a temperature that exists in a business setting or environment. Compare it to the temperature of the atmosphere. Human beings on this planet have adapted to certain temperature ranges. Similarly, employees need to survive and they therefore adapt themselves to the integrity and ethical levels they find in the work environment around them.

The question that still dogs me is whether the conscience of a single individual is divorced from the collective conscience of the organization. Is an organization justified in loading inflated costs on gullible clients? I haven't to date found the answer to that, and I am still searching. It is happening all around us. Airlines do it. Drug companies do it. What is the most effective way to align an individual's personal value system with that of the organization?

I saw what one unethical decision taken by a single entity could do. It could dilute the employees' faith in the organization. If someone on the client side figured it out, that would be the end of our reputation in the industry. I realized how important it is for the organization both to instill its value system into each employee down to the last level and to keep a check on whether it is being practiced.

When I joined the company, I was put through a rigorous training program including software quality and also a few sessions on the value system of the organization. But while it had high standards for maintaining software quality and rigorous checks for the same, it had no similar system in place for testing whether the value system was being practiced or not. I feel that organizations need equally rigorous processes for the implementation of their value systems.

■ Student #6: The B2B Strategy Challenge

In the spring of 2000, business-to-business (B2B) Internet ventures were the focus of many major corporations. Drawn by the tremendous amount of venture capital and ambitious analyst forecasts, many established CEOs and executives were looking for online opportunities to bridge buyers, suppliers, and manufacturers. At this time, I was a senior consultant with a recently public e-business consultancy. I worked in a ten-person strategy consulting group that provided business planning, financial, operational, and marketing advice to a broad range of start-ups.

Realizing this opportunity, a managing director and I had recently launched a new offering—B2B strategy consulting.

Executive officers from a large Real Estate Investment Trust (REIT) offered us a $300,000 contract to develop the business plan for a new, Internet-based business offering. I served as the day-to-day project lead, managing a team of analysts. My managing director would review our work one day a week. During the first week of the project, our team reviewed the market the REIT was targeting. Quickly, we realized the size of the prospective market could not sustain the enterprise it wanted to launch. As well, the proposed business had minimal opportunity to expand to other markets or offerings.

Our team was now at a crossroads. We could continue to write a business plan for an enterprise that we believed was not viable—and collect our $300,000 in fees. Alternatively, we could be honest with our client and communicate our early findings, consequently losing 95 percent of the contract revenues.

Personally, I struggled with a variety of issues. On one hand, our firm and division had revenue targets and fiscal responsibilities to our investors. Through this project, we could meet 33 percent of our group's targets. If we turned down this contract, it could put our numbers at risk. Alternatively, since my first day as a consultant, my mentors had emphasized one motto: "The client comes first." Our principal role was to serve the best interests of our clients. I was taught that a consulting firm's long-term success was built on the success stories of our clients. If we did not communicate our concerns to the client, we would be compromising our roles as objective advisers and putting their company at risk.

Outcome

Ultimately, my managing director and I were able to resolve this dilemma by considering the principles upon which our consulting group was founded, our professional experiences, and our inherent sense of morality. Several former consultants and investment bankers had founded our division. We all had different reasons for leaving our prior jobs to build this strategy consulting group. One theme, though, was consistent throughout—we enjoyed being trusted advisers to growing companies. We truly believed that we could maximize our long-term financial gain by serving the best interests of our customers. We were wary of quick wins that could compromise our long-term vision or operating principles. Finally, we relied on our gut reaction. Based on our own sense of morality, what did we believe was the ethical decision?

Consequently, the decision was easy. We were not willing to put the future of our firm at risk in the interest of meeting our short-term targets. We knew that we could face pressure from a variety of parties if we missed our quarterly targets. However, we believed that continuing this project would do greater damage to our reputation, as well as compromise our own sense of ethics. Our firm's management quickly supported our decision. When we presented our findings to our customer's representatives, they canceled the remainder of the contract, as we expected. However, we had gained the trust of a prominent client. This case was aggressively marketed in our future proposals. It helped us build a trusted brand that carried us through our acquisition by a major company in the fall of 2000.

TPOV

From this experience, I discovered the significant responsibility that management has in driving ethical decisions throughout a corporation. Even though I had my own sense of morality to fall back on, it was the core set of values established by our founders that had the greatest influence on my decision. In a corporate environment, you face different dilemmas than you do in your personal life. In personal decisions, you rely on the influences of your family, friends, and mentors to shape your decision. In corporate settings, managers, colleagues, and executives take on these same roles.

Our management empowered each employee to think freely and to make personal decisions. They preached that our primary goal was to serve the interests of our customers—and through this we would maximize our revenues and profits. They recruited employees who actively practiced these values.

Integrity in business is a function of a broad range of influences. From your birth, your family, friends, and teachers instill in you a core set of moral values. In business, management and colleagues help you apply these core values. As result, it is critical that management and founders establish and practice a core set of ethical priorities throughout an organization.

An entire organization must be recruited that believes in these priorities. That makes it safe and reasonable to empower employees to make difficult decisions. Employees and management can support one another in making these decisions. As well, they can challenge one another when they feel their core personal or corporate values are being compromised.

Exercises in Ethics

Here are the exercises our incoming MBAs completed. Work through them and develop your own answers.

1. What is the biggest ethical dilemma you have experienced in your career?

_____

_____

_____

_____

_____

_____

2. How did you respond?

_____

_____

_____

_____

_____

_____

_____

_____

_____

_____

_____

_____

_____

_____

3. What was the outcome?

_____

_____

_____

_____

_____

_____

_____

_____

_____

_____

_____

_____

_____

_____

4. How did (or does) that experience contribute to your Teachable Point of View on business ethics?

_____

_____

_____

_____

_____

_____

_____

_____

_____

_____

_____

_____

_____

5. If you haven't already done so, incorporate that learning into your Teachable Point of View on business ethics.

_____

_____

_____

_____

_____

_____

_____

_____

_____

_____

_____

_____

_____

16

Ethical Markets Are Essential for Trust, Global Development

E. LaBrent Chrite
Managing Director
William Davidson Institute
University of Michigan Business School

□

Editors' Note: Creating equitable capital markets is a critical growth step for developing countries around the world. Most fail. In part, this is because there are no institutions of market oversight, but even more, it's because expectations of corruption cause potential investors not to trust the market. The losses from such ethical wrongs can undo most of the good that can come from development. Occasionally, though, a country gets it right—as the African nation of Botswana has, by forming public-private partnerships and working for the long-term good. Not surprisingly, ethical nations tend to prosper.

The development of emerging economies, where about 85 percent of the world's population resides, can swing dramatically on the basis of ethics and corporate social responsibility.

One critical ingredient in the success of developing countries is the availability of investment capital. The creation of stock markets in developing countries, thus, can play a key, pivotal role.

But these countries also offer extraordinary challenges in the form of ethical dilemmas. And because they lack oversight bodies such as the U.S. Securities and Exchange Commission, they are rife with opportunities for corruption and mismanagement. And when government officials or businesspeople succumb to the temptation to fill their own pockets at the expense of investors, the markets are severely crippled.

Not only does such corruption detract from the much-needed private capital flow in these countries but, even more pernicious, it can breed cynicism and contempt on the part of the public as to what the role and benefits of private capital can be.

In developing stock markets, corruption and unethical behavior often have an important and exponential impact that can negate any development and growth that otherwise occurs in the nation.

More important than defining what's right, the first step toward getting it right is the process that a country's leaders employ and the evolution of decisions about the creation of a local capital market. This constitutes a means to achieving what's right through a public–private sector partnership. The most important thing in setting those standards is aligning the incentives with the reality of the marketplace.

■ Leadership and Governance Are Critical

Leadership and governance provide the predominant factor behind the dissonance or variance in progress seen across developing countries. Sound leadership and governance resulted in the highly productive economies of Eastern Europe and Southeast Asia, for instance, compared to what we see in Africa and parts of Latin America today, where the incentives are very different. Finding the right leadership and aligning a policy environment consistent with a thriving private sector is a major challenge. We don't see it succeed very often without getting the right folks to the table, when we can begin to create the right incentives and impetus.

It's similar to a country's Customs service. When system participation is erratic and people see many ways to cheat and pay off individuals instead of turning in the required amounts, or where they are required to make side payments to use the system at all, they are unlikely to do what is in the best interest of economic development, trust, use, and reliance on the system. Such disincentives mean you lose revenue streams, you lose good will, you stray from your stakeholders, and you create an environment that is volatile and without notions of fairness.

New stock markets can similarly follow suit—and that's precisely the reason that people need to come to the table together, to understand and align national policy with private sector goals and objectives. These must include everything from human capital development to ideas of how to manage and run each business.

Some developing countries have done this better than others. Most of my work is in sub-Saharan Africa, where a couple of countries have really set a precedent for logical or transparent public policies, for respect of the rule of law, and for recognizing the potential national benefits of competitiveness and quality of life, and have provided good stewardship for development.

In economic growth, for instance—and it's almost unprecedented—over the last twenty years Botswana has had the highest rate of continuing growth in the world. Botswana—in Africa!

What we've heard about over the last ten years is China, because of its population, obviously. But in the meantime, Botswana has grown steadily at 7.5 percent for two decades because of the positive environment there and because of its storehouse of natural resources. It can be done. Unfortunately, it's just one country out of fifty-four on the African subcontinent. But it does give us hope.

Clearly, when you think of entrepreneurial activity in many parts of the globe, the spillovers, externalities, and benefits can take place over the long run.

■ Outside Exploiters Can Degrade Markets

The world has seen scores of so-called secondary stock markets start up to attract investments from common citizens, only to have the money taken by early outsider investors, who then bail out of the country with the money.

When others come in to make such short-term gains and exploit the community, they degrade the environment, take out local capital, and never look back. And when that's what people see, that's unfortunately what they equate to capitalism.

Similarly, they see examples of U.S. corruption at Enron, WorldCom, and the rest as an opportunity to suggest that Americans not be so quick to point fingers.

Some seem to be saying that, "Maybe now the U.S. will realize that it's not perfect, and maybe the U.S. will now realize it's not just us."

It's not just the U.S. financial scandals. The 2000 U.S. presidential election results caused Zimbabwe's President Robert Mugabe, who has been implicated in the manipulation of an election or two in his own right, to volunteer to come to America from Africa to help with the vote-counting.

Cynical, to be sure.

But it is symbolic of what many people around the world are saying as they see ethical wrongs in the United States, "Look, we don't wish ill upon anybody, but, you know, maybe you all need to be humbled a bit."

In the end, we can hope, that such introspection can lead to better functioning and more transparent capital markets in the United States and the world.

Exercises in Ethics

Ethical dilemmas extend to countries and their capital markets, often targets of corruption in the early days of development.

1. Think about the developing countries (or even areas in developed regions) where your firm does or could conduct business. List the most significant ones across the top of the following chart:

Countries

Public-private partnership with goal alignment	____	____	____	____	____
Incentives aligned with marketplace realities	____	____	____	____	____
Sound leadership and governance	____	____	____	____	____
Transparent public policies	____	____	____	____	____
Respect for rule of law	____	____	____	____	____
Recognition of potential national benefits of competition	____	____	____	____	____

2. Place an "X" in the cell for each country that you would rate "good" or better on each of the dimensions of the chart on the previous page.

3. For country columns lacking a preponderance of X's, how do you explain the value of conducting business there?

_____

_____

_____

_____

_____

_____

4. Explain the value of conducting business in these countries from the standpoint of ethics and integrity.

_____

_____

_____

_____

_____

_____

5. Incorporate this rationale for conducting business in developing countries into your Teachable Point of View on business ethics.

_____

_____

_____

_____

_____

_____

_____

17

Living Beautiful Values Every Day Makes Focus: HOPE Special

Eleanor Josaitis
Co-Founder and Executive Director
Focus: HOPE

Editors' Note: Focus: HOPE is simply one of a kind—the single best place in the world for developing people to achieve more than they ever thought possible. For three decades a role model for treating people with dignity and respect, Focus: HOPE gets the most out of its inner-city candidates by providing grand opportunities while holding people to the highest standards and demanding excellence. Here, co-founder Eleanor Josaitis addresses University of Michigan Business School incoming MBAs after they spent the day in global citizenship activities at Focus: HOPE and other community organizations around the state.

You're fantastic.

The grand Corporate Global Citizenship work by Michigan's MBAs today at Focus: HOPE and elsewhere mean more than you will ever know.

For all the groups that you helped, they will never stop thanking you. And to the teams that came out to Focus: HOPE, thank you from the bottom of my heart. You made a difference— and we're grateful.

You're all very, very talented and gifted men and women and I love your commitment—the fact that you want to give back to the community, that you're going to share no matter where you go or where your journey takes you.

I want to tell you, you never know where your journey's going to take you.

I was a suburban housewife, raising five children, living a very comfortable life. But I can tell you of the exact moment when my life changed. I was sitting in my living room watching the Nuremberg trials on television—absolutely appalled by what I was seeing. The program was interrupted by the march in Mississippi. And I sat there and watched as policemen were riding through, giving electric shocks with cattle prods, turning fire hoses loose on the marchers, dogs flipping little kids in the air.

I cried my eyes out. And I kept asking myself, what would I have done if I had lived in Germany during the time all the horrible things brought out in the Nuremburg trials took place? Would I have pretended I didn't see anything? Would I have become involved? What would I have done?

It changed me just like that.

I became a very strong supporter of Dr. Martin Luther King Jr. And Father William Cunningham, who was my friend, was also a very strong King supporter. When the riots hit Detroit in 1967, Father Cunningham and I came together and said we had to do something.

He was an English professor who quit his teaching profession and took over the Madonna parish in the heart of the city. My husband and I sold our home and moved into an integrated neighborhood in the heart of the city—because I was not about to ask anybody to do anything I wasn't willing to do myself.

■ Family Thought She "Flipped Out"

My mother hired an attorney to take my five children away from me. My father-in-law disowned us. And my brother-in-law, who was an engineer, asked me to please use my maiden name so I wouldn't embarrass the family. It wasn't because they didn't love me. They thought I had flipped out. My youngest was three. My oldest was eleven. And the family couldn't understand why I would want to do something like this.

That made me a stronger person, made me even more determined. And I had even more passion in my heart to keep going.

My mother changed. She became a very strong supporter. And my brother-in-law—he now thinks I'm cool, so we're over that.

□

I learned a lot of lessons along the way. I can close my eyes and see the same scene that I saw thirty-five years ago. And it's still in my heart today. We wrote a mission statement that hangs on all the walls at Focus: HOPE and is on the back of all our business cards.

It reads: "Recognizing the dignity and beauty of every person, we pledge intelligent and practical action to overcome racism, poverty, and injustice, to build a metropolitan community where all people may live in freedom, harmony, trust and affection—black and white, yellow, brown, and red, from Detroit and its suburbs, of every economic status, national origin, religious persuasion, we join in this covenant. March 8th, 1968."

Today some people are surprised that we still have that same mission statement. I'll say, "Do you think we've achieved it? Do you think we've built a world where we all appreciate one another, where everybody has opportunities and options in their life?"

This is the human capital business.

The first thing we did was listen to the people in the city talk about being ripped off in city supermarkets. We got five hundred volunteers in the city, five hundred volunteers in the suburbs, did a very sophisticated survey—in all the mom-and-pop shops, the independent stores—went in and took down all the prices. We fed the data through the computers at Chrysler Corporation and found that folks in the city were paying 30 percent to 40 percent more for their groceries, and that the chain stores were dumping the old meat and old produce from the suburbs into the city.

As a result, it went on national television—twenty-eight managers were fired for ripping people off.

The people in the suburbs said, "We didn't know this was happening."

People in the city said, "We've been trying to tell you it's happening."

They came together and said, "What do you want us to do next, Focus: HOPE?"

Meanwhile, we were listening to the scientific community talk about babies losing their brainpower if they didn't have food in the first three years of their life. An infant will lose 15 percent of its brainpower in the first three years, if it does not have all the food that its body commands. Fifteen percent!

■ Roots of National Food Program

We thought it was intelligent and practical to start a food program. We designed it for pregnant women, nursing mothers, children up to the age of six—because if the family was still in need, the older ones could get the school lunch and the school breakfast program.

Now here comes lesson Number one—big-time lesson. I got a telephone call one day from a woman—she was whispering into the phone—and kept saying, "Mrs. Josaitis, I understand you have food."

I went rattling off about this fabulous program for pregnant women, mothers, children, and on and on. I'm bragging about the program. And there was a long pause.

Then she screamed into the phone at me, "I am seventy-two years old and you want me to get pregnant before you'll help me?"

She told me off—laid me flat on the ground. I had it coming to me. The lesson she taught me is that I heard every single word the woman said. But I did not hear her fear. She was living on $308 a month in a neighborhood that was totally disintegrated. She didn't give a hoot in hell what we were doing, she wanted somebody to listen to her fear. I picked myself off the floor.

I said, "Father, let's change the regulations. Let's add seniors to our food program." We hired two researchers, had enough data to fill this building, and off to Washington we went—saying, "Please may we change the regulations?"

We testified before members of the House and the Senate thirty-two times. Five years later, we were still sitting at the table, pleading for food.

Here comes lesson Number two: We were sitting there one day, pleading for food before the Senate. The meanest man I ever met in my life was sitting on the other side of me. He was then the Secretary of Agriculture [Earl Butz]. He'd just dumped thousands of gallons of milk down the sewers of Los Angeles, rather than give it to poor people.

The man brought out so much rage in me that if I'd had any instrument in my hand, I'd have done bodily harm to him.

Michigan Senator Phil Hart recognized my frustration and when the hearing was over, he motioned to me. He took me downstairs to the Senate cafeteria, put his hand across the table, and said, "Honey, if you would've gone for his jugular vein like you were going to, you'd have gone to the slammer and he would've won. . . . You've got to learn to outsmart him."

I did. I came back and borrowed an airplane from Ford Motor Company and flew to Washington, picked up all the legislative directors, Department of Agriculture officials, and brought them here, put them on buses, drove them all through the city. They went away saying they understood.

That food program is now a national law—the Commodities Supplemental Food Program for Mothers, Children, and Seniors. It's in thirty-two states. Last month, Focus: HOPE provided food to 42,608 people.

I cannot wait until the day when I can close off the street, hire a Dixieland band, and celebrate because nobody has to be on a food program any more.

■ Moving into the Financial Mainstream

But let's deal with reality. How do you get people off food programs? How do you get them into the financial mainstream? How do you provide jobs for them? How do you break down racial barriers so people have opportunities in their life? That's what we're about.

We started the Machinist Training Institute because of the 487 business owners we interviewed, only two had ever hired a minority or woman. Two out of 487! We started the Machinist Training Institute to break the racial barrier. We've started the Information Technology Center. Break the barrier. Get people into jobs. Child-care center—the greatest gift I can give my colleagues and the community. You don't have to worry about your little people. You can walk in there, 140 little kids going through Montessori school. This can provide opportunities for mom and dad—and they don't have to worry about their little one.

Our engineering program is working like a charm. Our young men and women are now invited all over—they're going to Europe, they're traveling, they recognize that globalization is here. They're prepared.

The moral of the story is: You don't know where your journey will take you. Keep your mind and your heart open.

I want to close by sharing my "love letters" with you. I got two at exactly the same time.

One's in a Focus: HOPE envelope, so I head for that one. The other one says: "Enclosed please find a check in the amount of $10,000. This is to help you continue the good work that Father Cunningham and you started. We need more organizations like yours in the world."

Made me feel pretty good.

The other letter: "I wish I could stop your Focus: HOPE news. Thirty-six years of n****-bashing us whites like I was called, you damn white s***** honky, we're tired of you free-loading n****. Shape up you lousy welfare n****. Thirty-six years of you, we've had it."

Here's one that didn't have a note or a letter or anything—just had a dollar bill in it.

We all remember 9/11. On 9/11, I called all of my colleagues together—all six hundred. And I said, "Can you continue to be an ambassador from a civil and human rights point of view? Can you continue to judge your brothers and sisters on the content of their character? Can you continue to strive to build a world that we all want to live in?"

All six hundred of them signed on immediately.

I wrote a letter to the editor, on the editorial page of the *Detroit Free Press,* with a headline that said, "Strive to Build a World That Embraces Diversity."

And the letter that I received back again on the back of that article says, "Shove diversity up your a** b****."

Does anybody think I'm going to be intimidated for one minute by this?

It is only going to make me work harder. Our mission is too important.

Exercises in Ethics

In doing what is morally and ethically right, Eleanor Josaitis is energized by her detractors as she builds Focus: HOPE into a model for human development and respect.

1. Corporate citizenship often presents similar obstacles to companies—obstacles that do not deter leaders with integrity who have made commitments to improve their communities.

   a. What are your own commitments to corporate citizenship?

   _____

   _____

   _____

_____

_____

_____

_____

_____

_____

_____

b. Why do you feel keeping these commitments is important?

_____

_____

_____

_____

_____

_____

_____

_____

_____

2. Incorporate your corporate citizenship commitments and the rationale for why they are important into your Teachable Point of View on business ethics.

_____

_____

_____

_____

_____

_____

_____

_____

_____

18

Corporate Global Citizenship

The Ethical Path for Business

Noel M. Tichy, Andrew R. McGill
Professors of Organizational Behavior and Human Resource Management University of Michigan Business School

□

A fundamental business ethic that writing and editing this book has reinvigorated in us is the importance of corporate global citizenship. We have written on this topic at length in the past (*Corporate Global Citizenship: Doing Business in the Public Eye*, New Lexington Press, 1997). In fact, that book included early and detailed insights about Enron and its questionable power-generation practices in India.

But, more important, it detailed early and dramatically successful examples of businesses and their leaders in corporate global citizenship activities. It is difficult to think of a more important basic business ethical commitment than to be a good citizen in the world of your business—with real involvement of your people, as well as your money.

One lesson from the Teachable Point of View process for us is that leaders worth their salt must also be highly visible as dedicated global citizens and teach others about it. The stakes in maintaining the stability of both the social and physical environment and the benefits of community engagement are too great to be overlooked. Companies that ignore them will fall behind those that don't. And to be on the winning side, all leaders must develop a TPOV on how they will be personally engaged—and on how they will get the corporation as an institution and their people within it engaged, too.

Successful business leaders at all levels must be engaged as good citizens to bring their wisdom to help wrestle with global challenges and resolve disparities like these:

The GDP of the developed world—the United States, European Community, and Japan, with a combined total population of about 750 million—is more than $23 trillion. The rest of the world, including China with 1.2 billion people and India with about 1 billion people, lives on less than $3 trillion in GDP. The world's five largest companies—GE, ExxonMobil, Microsoft, Pfizer, and Wal-Mart—have a market capitalization bigger than the GDP of India.

■ Global Corporations Must Play Big Role

In the twenty-first century, we live in a world where global corporations must play a role in dealing with corporate citizenship
issues and resource inequalities. These include the environmental issues of toxic pollution, global warming, depletion of non-
renewable resources, and loss of biodiversity, as well as the
human issues of distribution of wealth, nutrition, health, housing, and education.

It's time leaders at all levels understand and prepare to ac-
cept several basic principles:

- Businesses operate in a global community and have global
  obligations.
- Giving money isn't enough; active participation in the community is essential.
- Community volunteerism hones leadership skills for individuals, the company, and the community, while providing
  opportunities for learning.
- Citizenship activities energize workers and build bonds.

Citizenship activities can reinforce the ethical commitments
of both leader and organization, putting faces, voices, and perspectives on some of the most challenging dilemmas in life.

But, a priori, business leaders must cleanse their own house
first.

To sustain a healthy free-enterprise system, capital markets
must have transparency and trust in the system. Changes in the
regulatory apparatus can diminish the likelihood that certain
egregious behaviors will recur, but new rules and new regulators are only a piece of the solution. No society can legislate
morality. The other part of rebuilding trust and confidence is the
more important part: Developing world-class leaders with unyielding integrity, leaders who will transform their organizations

and develop a new generation of leaders. Without such leadership, our free-enterprise society may be undermined.

When GE's Jeffrey Immelt became CEO, for instance, he was dealt a hand that not only included the world's most valuable enterprise and most respected company but also a foundation for GE corporate citizenship dating back to 1928. That's when GE's Elfun Society was founded to foster "loyalty, fellowship, cooperation, innovations and resourcefulness among GE's managers." The society was set up to achieve its goals internally and to make a difference in local communities—and has been in operation ever since, with a long legacy of success.

During the Welch era, the Elfun Society grew to about forty thousand members—about half retirees, the rest professionals and managers. Welch encouraged them to be active and to rededicate themselves, "rallying Elfun around the concept of volunteerism and taking advantage of the tremendous GE retirement team, which can truly make a difference in each community where we live and work."

In 1992, the Elfuns began expanding globally, forming new chapters in Japan, Singapore, Malaysia, Mexico, Brazil, the United Kingdom, the Netherlands, and Hungary, which joined the previously established chapters in Puerto Rico and Canada. The society anticipates further expansion as GE businesses increase operations and staffing around the world.

Elfun's aim throughout the 1990s was to expand partnerships with public schools and other community service organizations.

■ CEO Wants GE to Do Much More

Immelt and his senior team, inheritors of this platform, are strong believers in Elfun. But even though the new CEO believes Elfun has made a difference, as he looks to the future, he says GE must do more—a lot more—to promote healthy societies.

Tichy was talking with Immelt as he prepared for his first officers' meeting in the fall of 2001 when news came to his office that an NBC employee had tested positive for anthrax. Sitting at Welch's old round table, Immelt said:

> In the past, it's been that as long as our stock was good, we were the most admired company. But I think the world demands more today. I'd given this a lot of thought before 9/11, but now it takes on a new meaning.
>
> Fundamentally, GE's my life. This company is all I think about. It's who I am. Twenty years ago, here's what Jack saw. Here's what he did, and, you know what? We got a better place. Today, here's what I see—and it's not enough. GE's great, but not great enough. . . . We have to be a more important company. We have to be a more vocal company on causes. We have to stand for something more than the value of the stock price.
>
> I'm trying to do this in a very respectful way, but also set a new trajectory. . . . We are the best and we've proven that, and Jack handed us the best company. That's the hand I was dealt. But in tomorrow's world, that is not enough. It can't be paternalistic. It has nothing to do with paternalism. . . .
>
> The first thing is, this has got to be a place where people are put first, people are treated with respect. Start with people. You know, it's going to be people, including the community— I've been a little bit hesitant to really go all the way here, but now that 9/11 has happened, I am absolutely certain.

Immelt was right to say GE needs to do more. Just as Peter Drucker was right in saying that the world depends on companies like GE doing their part.

In legal terms, corporations have many of the same rights and privileges as individuals. They also have many of the same obligations, including the duty to be good citizens. But, as Drucker says, people need more: "Individuals—and especially knowledge workers—need an additional sphere of life, of personal relationships, and of contribution outside and beyond the job, outside and beyond the organization, indeed, outside and beyond their own specialized knowledge area."

One organization that embodies the essence of integrating values and ethics in business is ServiceMaster—a sterling example. We deeply appreciate its contribution over the years in trying to get the ethics item on the agenda with business and business education, as well as its important contribution to this book by underwriting the 2002 Hansen-Wessner Lecture, which brought former Secretary of State James A. Baker III to the University of Michigan Business School. Unfortunately, ServiceMaster's high emphasis on ethics remains a business aberration in both reality and perception.

It's pretty disappointing to pick up the *Wall Street Journal* and see that most business executives are held in the lowest esteem in society—in all the time they've been doing this polling. The tremendous impact—the fallout from Enron, WorldCom, and the rest, plus other events have given us a great opportunity to reflect.

■ Multiple Benefits Flow from Teaching

The exciting news about all of this is that our experience over the last twenty years clearly indicates that business leaders and employees generally get multiple benefits from engaging in Virtuous Teaching Cycles with the community, not the least of which is adding to the esprit de corps of the company. Giving back through volunteering turbocharges the workforce. When people feel good about themselves and their companies for supporting such activities, they are generally energized to work harder for the company, as well.

We have seen it over and over again—working in inner-city homeless shelters or food programs or mentoring programs gives people a renewed perspective on their own lives and the blessings that they have in life. This carries over into the workplace, putting some of the day-to-day problems and frictions of work life in a new perspective. It also opens the door to a new place to learn about leadership, stewardship, and the effective use of resources.

"Volunteering in the community is an incredibly powerful teaching and learning experience for the organization," says Len Schlesinger, COO of Limited Brands. "We are working to make sure that people understand that their volunteer leadership roles are, in fact, leadership roles."

What it really comes down to are the principles that underlie teaching organizations. It is through teaching and learning that people grow. People who leave the comfort zones of their familiar environments and go out into the world learn more and become smarter than people who don't. So it isn't just about writing checks and making donations. Those are important things to do. But people don't learn, don't get excited, and don't develop strong commitments to check-writing. What really makes a difference, for donors and—we would argue—for the recipients as well, is the face-to-face interaction.

Even for the recipients of the aid, the learning and the growth are primary benefits. In emergency situations, the need to provide immediate food, shelter, health care, and support services may take precedence over meaningful personal interchanges. But solving problems over the longer term, so that crises are less likely to occur, depends on people with resources working with the people most affected by the problems—to come up with solutions. This requires spending time together and a mutual openness to teaching and learning.

Les Wexner of Limited Brands, for example, has started a program to get every kindergartner and first grader in Ohio together with a tutor. The single best predictor for who will graduate from high school, he says, is mastering reading in the first grade. So Wexner is enlisting volunteers across the state, starting with employees of Limited Brands.

"Les has always been actively engaged on a personal level, but until recently, he was reluctant to push others in the company," says COO Schlesinger. But now he has a Teachable Point of View that says, "Being good citizens is what makes this company different. We are over being uncomfortable and are being clear that community service is an expectation."

■ Leaders Must Develop Community Plan

The communities, the abilities that reside in a company, and the interests of its people will differ. The job of the leader, however, is to develop a plan and an action agenda around community service and to make sure that it is taken seriously within the company.

We believe that business leaders must engage with their communities in a much more creative and profound way than ever before. Partnerships with government cannot be lobbying efforts for self-interests.

Global issues cannot be put off as "beggar thy neighbor" problems. We are all interconnected. Those in the developed world can control their own destinies only by engaging in long-term global citizenship issues. The stakeholders go well beyond Wall Street and the customer. They include the free enterprise system itself and the societies in which businesses operate throughout the planet.

When we take business executives to work at Focus: HOPE in Detroit, for instance, they are regularly blown away with how much can be done with such small resources, and how mission- and value-driven organizations can mobilize thousands of people with no financial compensation.

On a budget of less than $70 million, Focus: HOPE feeds more than forty thousand people a month, trains machinists and engineers, and runs a fast-track high school program as well as a children's center and several for-profit machine tool businesses.

Lloyd Reuss was so impressed with it that after he retired as president of General Motors he became executive dean of Focus: HOPE's Center for Advanced Technologies. Chief Operating Officer Tim Duperron took early retirement as a Ford executive to work there. Keith Cooley of GM followed suit.

We are so impressed with Focus: HOPE and its leaders that we have brought more than forty thousand business leaders to do volunteer work there over the decades. These have included groups from companies such as Ameritech, Ford, Hewlett-Packard, and Shell. In addition, we run MBA orientation sessions on leadership development at Focus: HOPE, and Noel Tichy personally spends as much as 20 percent of his time doing pro bono leadership development work with Eleanor Josaitis and her Focus: HOPE team.

But not all social service agencies are Focus: HOPE. Lacking the discipline of the marketplace, many nonprofits are notoriously ineffective and wasteful. The experience of being in one of these is often an eye-opener for executives to rethink how their own operations run. The shortcomings in the volunteer agencies that are so obvious to them as outsiders are sometimes not all that far from shortcomings they have been unable or unwilling to see in their own organizations.

Despite some highly publicized examples of self-dealing, greed, and downright dishonesty in major nonprofits, they can't compete with American business in the early 2000s—and, most often, inefficiencies in the nonprofits primarily reflect a lack of business acumen on the part of poorly trained staff and volunteers. In these situations, corporate leaders often have expertise that would be helpful. But delivering this expertise requires a big commitment of time, as well as some finely honed leadership skills.

That's because in the dynamic of most nonprofits, the professional staff is expected to take the lead, while the volunteers drop in to be the followers. Focus: HOPE has successfully blended this norm. But it is a very tricky proposition when a volunteer has more expertise than the agency's staff. To teach and transmit that knowledge effectively, the volunteer first has to establish credibility, and then to communicate in a way that doesn't threaten the staffers and make them shut down.

These are essential leadership skills. Putting them to work this way in volunteer activities helps both the volunteer and the agency.

But this kind of interaction is never going to happen if the potential volunteer remains in the corporate office, writing checks and never becoming a volunteer.

While ongoing, long-term relationships such as those between Hewlett-Packard and East Palo Alto's OICW and Cisco's support of thousands of inner-city school programs to teach "Cisco Networking" skills are certainly the most productive, even brief half-day encounters can be valuable if they are well thought out.

Over the years, we have probably put more than two hundred thousand students and executives to work in various community service projects. These ranged from a one-day cleanup of a park to painting a halfway house in London to Habitat for Humanity projects to ongoing tutoring programs in Chicago, New York, and Detroit. Even though many were one-time community service events, a significant number, about 20 percent, evolved into ongoing programs that continued over multiple years.

These include a Focus: HOPE volunteer program with Ford employees delivering food monthly to seniors, Saturday morning reading programs in Chicago by Ameritech managers, and annual Habitat for Humanity fundraising and volunteering by the Michigan MBAs.

Doug Hoover, a senior executive at EDS, went back from a
service event and mobilized hundreds of his colleagues to work
in the community. He personally gives a lot of time to Focus:
HOPE. An executive from Otsuka Pharmaceuticals in Japan vis-
ited an AIDS clinic in Washington, D.C. with us, and then went
back to Japan and altered some of the company's research and
development to increase its focus on AIDS drugs. It was the result of the Virtuous Teaching Cycle created when he actually sat
down with a dying AIDS patient that made the difference. For
years he had been working on R&D for an AIDS drug for the
company, but had never actually met anyone with the disease.

■ The Global Leadership Program

Another example of how this can work in even a very short time
frame are our citizenship visits with senior executives in our
Michigan Global Leadership Program to Clean and Sober Streets
in Washington, D.C. The GLP was a five-week action-learning
experience that brought together teams of Japanese, American,
and European leaders from major corporations. The primary action-learning vehicle was country assessments in China, India,
Russia, and Brazil, based on extended interviewing and reporting in those countries. The program began with team building
at the Outward Bound School on Hurricane Island, Maine, then
moved on for a day in Washington, D.C.

The purpose of the day in Washington was to hone the students' skills at diagnosing community issues such as poverty,
racism, drugs, health care shortfalls, and the like, and to get
them to begin wrestling with some tough leadership questions.
These included how they would shape their own leadership
agendas when they returned to their companies.

Clean and Sober Streets is a residential drug rehabilitation
center attached to the Mitch Snyder Homeless Shelter, one of the

largest in the country, and its clients are some of the hardest-core addicts in the city. To be admitted to the program, a person must have been on drugs for many years.

We began by having our thirty executives arrive at 6 A.M. to help prepare breakfast for the residents. Then they ate breakfast with the residents. Everyone sat at round cafeteria tables, with three executives and three residents at each. Our group included VPs from Sony, Honda, Merck, IBM, Exxon, and Nokia, among others. The format was for each table to discuss a series of questions. It started with everyone telling their own life stories and what led to them being seated at the table. In several cases, the formative years were not that different for executive or resident—the pivotal event for the latter being when they crossed into addiction. The group then moved on to talking about their aspirations, and finally, each executive had to offer each resident at the table a piece of concrete advice.

It may sound superficial, but the one-to-one human connections really did make a difference to both the executives and the residents. The executives were pulled way out of their comfort zones—forced to see a side of life that was totally foreign to them. And the residents, even though the visit was short, had the benefit of having the complete and focused attention of people with brains and resources whom they would otherwise never meet.

Nobody was under any illusion that the residents were going to get it together to save money and go to college. All of them were addicts, many had felony records, and 60 percent were HIV-positive. So the executives had to learn a whole new way of thinking—as someone trying to get into the system from the bottom instead of as a member of the elite, for whom doors and paths easily open.

The advice they came up with wasn't exactly startling. It included such things as how to get rid of street talk, what to wear and why, how to deal with a felony past, and what skills were worth developing at Clean and Sober Streets. But the comments carried extra weight because they were directed at the specific individual resident. They weren't just generic platitudes but personal messages that were taken more seriously.

By the end of the several-hour breakfast, everyone was chattering like old friends—which is important in itself. Similarly, Eleanor Josaitis of Focus: HOPE has a policy of having her students line up to shake hands with visiting executives. The reason for doing this, she says, "has nothing to do with the executives. It has to do with my students' pride and dignity, their self-esteem, and claiming their place in society."

The session at Clean and Sober Streets was short, and we do not pretend to have made a world-shattering difference for the residents. But for these executives who have, or someday may have, stewardship over significant resources, it was an important step in their education about life. We left convinced that the residents of Clean and Sober Streets did get a direct benefit from their participation. But even those who didn't made important contributions to social improvement by serving as teachers and helping focus these future leaders on the reality of some significant social problems.

We ran the Global Leadership Program for ten years, through 1998. During that time, we engaged more than 250 executives from around the world in citizenship activities. We asked them to make a commitment to citizenship when they returned to their companies, but we knew that even with the best of intentions many of them would not follow through. When we followed up, however, we were happy to discover that 50 percent actually kept their commitments. The projects we found included such things as engaging all their direct reports in inner-city tutoring, taking their teams to work at Habitat for Humanity sites, and running citizenship programs with community groups.

We challenged them each to develop a personal leadership agenda and action plan in this area. Then they turned to us on the faculty and said: "What are you doing at the Business School? You have a chance to shape the next generation of leaders. What are you doing with your MBA students?"

■ Global Citizenship for Michigan MBAs

So Michael Brimm from INSEAD in France started a program to engage INSEAD MBAs in global citizenship, and we began the citizenship program as part of Orientation for each incoming MBA student at Michigan.

Since 1990, all of the incoming MBAs at Michigan have spent two days in corporate citizenship activities with companies in the community. We started the program as the result of a Virtuous Teaching Cycle that we got going with the first class.

One group always goes to Focus: HOPE. Another section of seventy students goes to Benton Harbor to work with Whirlpool in community development in an inner-city environment outside the headquarters area. When we gather back on campus, we then open up a conversation to challenge the students to think about what citizenship means for them personally, what it means for business, and whether they will stay involved.

When Noel Tichy proposed the program, colleagues at the business school were reluctant, saying that community service would potentially turn off incoming MBAs who were, after all, "money-focused capitalists, not social workers." The reality has been 180 degrees different. The students love it, and a full 70 percent stay involved doing community volunteer work during their MBA experience. Global corporate citizenship is now a core part of the Michigan MBA leadership development experience.

This got us to realize the need to integrate community service as an element of leadership development in every institution, every organization, with every client. The results have been gratifying. Since 1990, all of our leadership development experiences have involved at least a half-day in community service, as part of both their team building and leadership development.

When we cascade leadership development throughout a company, we require executives and leaders at all levels to run three-day workshops. For a half-day of this, they take their teams out to the community, both to engage in the community and to learn from it. At Ameritech, we took thirty thousand people out for half-day community service projects and thousands of them became volunteers afterward.

In the mid-1990s, Ford required the top two thousand leaders to take more than a hundred thousand people on half-day citizenship projects. The result of the activities around the world, from Beijing to Cologne to Dearborn, led Bill Ford and Jacques Nasser to allocate two days for paid community service for all salaried employees at Ford—140,000 of them. The caveat is the projects have to be team activities in which a group picks a project and goes out as a team. This was because they saw corporate citizenship as a team development activity as well as doing good.

Royal Dutch/Shell has likewise involved half of its hundred thousand employees worldwide in community service activities as part of its leadership development programs. US West, now part of Qwest, has implemented similar programs, as have a number of Silicon Valley high-tech firms.

The point here is that it never fails. Given the right leadership and the right opportunities, companies and the people within them benefit from engaging in the community. The key is to approach it as a Virtuous Teaching Cycle. Its purpose isn't to hand out charity but to create an opportunity for mutual teaching and learning.

■ Focus: HOPE, a Best-Practice Model

Focus: HOPE is a civil rights organization in inner-city Detroit that provides food for people and helps them acquire the education and skills to enter the economic mainstream. (See Chapter Seventeen for a first-person account of its origin and activities.) It's an organization with a thirty-five-year mission to look for intelligent and practical solutions to racism and poverty.

Because its primary mission is social activism, we are not holding it up as a role model for corporations and business executives to copy. But we want to underscore it as an example of how Virtuous Teaching Cycles can cross all kinds of boundaries—and to show just how effective community service activities can be.

Focus: HOPE, as Eleanor Josaitis reports in Chapter Seventeen, is a model of how partnerships with the community, government, business, universities, and foundations can create meaningful change for both individuals and the community. It serves as a challenge to our imaginations as to what is possible—and a catalyst for creative thinking.

Focus: HOPE grew out of the 1967 Detroit race riots. At the time, Father William Cunningham was a young Roman Catholic priest teaching English at Sacred Heart Seminary. As Army Airborne units came to the rescue, he looked around and saw the poverty, rage, and despair that permeated the inner city's black neighborhoods and decided: "I can't keep teaching Beowulf and Shakespeare and English composition . . . with the choppers coming and the half-tracks and the 50-caliber machine guns turned on the side of buildings, and the encampment of Central High School . . . [I felt] we had to do something."

So he and Eleanor Josaitis started out with the determination to make a difference. Starting with the food program, each successive program they created took them deeper into the community. And as each program got up and running, Cunningham and Josaitis would look around to see what they could do better and what needs were going unfulfilled.

The success of the food program was a red flag. There were way too many hungry babies in Detroit. So they looked around for a way to reduce the need for food giveaways—and quickly saw that the children were hungry because their parents didn't have jobs. Cunningham and Josaitis decided that if they really wanted to have a long-term impact, they needed to help adults acquire the skills to find work—and not just entry-level work, but careers with upward mobility.

Since the biggest employer in Detroit is the auto industry, and some of the best-paying and most stable jobs were as machinists, Cunningham and Josaitis decided to teach inner-city workers not only to be machinists but to be some of the best machinists in the world. Focus: HOPE graduates would get and keep jobs not because socially conscious employers pitied them but because they would be solid, reliable workers with skills the employers needed. In the year 2003, entry-level pay for machinists averaged $13 an hour, making upward mobility very possible.

Once they started the machinist training program, they realized that people needed help with more basic skills. Even people who had graduated from Detroit public schools often didn't have the tenth-grade math and reading skills needed to succeed in the machinists' program. So they put together a FAST TRACK program to advance people through several grade levels of math and English in seven weeks, so they could apply for the machinist program, or go out into the market to look for other jobs. When they found that a lot of eager people weren't even ready for FAST TRACK, they started an even more basic program. When another big challenge surfaced over problems with child care—parents wanted to attend classes but had no one to care for their children—Focus: HOPE started a child care center and a Montessori school.

■ TPOV: Never Lower Your Standards

A very strong Teachable Point of View at Focus: HOPE is that you must never lower standards. If people are to succeed in the mainstream economy, they must be able to meet all of its demands. So to reinforce this, Focus: HOPE set up a for-profit machine shop, producing some of the highest-precision items required by customers such as Detroit Diesel, General Motors, Ford, and Chrysler. The test for the students is whether they can please the customers and keep them coming back—just like in the real world.

In 1993, with the support of the government, corporations, banks, and foundations, Cunningham and Josaitis opened the Center for Advanced Technologies (CAT), a 220,000-square-foot manufacturing and education facility. The former industrial engine plant—renovated at a cost of $22 million—now houses some of the most modern manufacturing equipment in the world. A coalition of five major manufacturing companies and five leading engineering universities joined Focus: HOPE to develop a world-class curriculum to educate "renaissance engineers." Three of those universities—Lawrence Technological University, Wayne State University, and the University of Detroit Mercy—award associate and bachelor's degrees to graduates of the CAT program in manufacturing engineering technology.

CAT's very novel curriculum includes both academic study and hands-on experience in a real-world manufacturing environment—producing engineers whose starting salaries can top $80,000, $4,000 to $5,000 above those of MIT grads. In large part, this is because of their hands-on experience in actual production and fulfillment of major industry contracts.

More important, Focus: HOPE programs have a strong work ethic and have Focus: HOPE's values about working with and developing others.

Focus: HOPE is truly a teaching organization. Everyone is responsible—no matter how much or how little time they've spent there—for teaching the people who are coming along behind them. It now totals about six hundred people, on a forty-acre campus, with a budget of nearly $70 million a year.

Father Cunningham died in 1997, but Eleanor Josaitis remains as the head teacher. At seventy years old, she walks the manufacturing and educational facilities every single morning starting around six—as she has for decades. She interviews every candidate who applies to work there to screen for values and emotional energy. And she lets them know the values of Focus: HOPE are for real.

■ Why Focus: HOPE Works

Over the years, we've concluded that Focus: HOPE is so successful because it incorporates a number of critical elements:

- *Grass roots:* The organization is based in the local community. Its leaders live in the community and are involved in the life of the community, so it is closely attuned to the real needs of the community.
- *Value-based mission:* The mission of Focus: HOPE is intelligent and practical solutions to racism and poverty.
- *Human dignity:* People are all valued whether they have been unemployed for forty years and are food program recipients or have graduated with a bachelor's degree and are starting a $50,000-a-year job. Everyone walks the walk on respecting the dignity of every human being.
- *Enlightened capitalism:* Focus: HOPE is built on a firm belief in capitalism. The goal is to give people opportunities to gain the mainstream economic values of living in a capitalist society. Yet Focus: HOPE will not refuse food to anyone in need.

There's a belief that it's not inconsistent to take care of people's true needs while holding them to high standards to perform in a capitalistic society.

- *Leadership at all levels:* Everyone is expected to lead, whether they've been at Focus: HOPE for one week or for twenty-five years. This is not a hierarchical organization but rather a group of colleagues, each leading to the best of their limits.
- *Virtuous Teaching Cycles at all levels:* Everybody tries to make everyone else smarter. Teaching and coaching occurs everywhere. Because of the values system and the approach of Focus: HOPE, there are illustrations of Virtuous Teaching Cycles all over the organization.
- *Boundaryless behavior:* Focus: HOPE has minimal hierarchical boundaries—and there is a great deal of movement across functional boundaries and program boundaries. People communicate, share best practices, and engage in community activities across the whole institution.
- *Knowledge generation:* Focus: HOPE is continuously trying to make itself and every one of its colleagues smarter. In its partnerships with universities and the business community, it is always looking for new information and best practices. For example, it surveys three hundred-plus machine-tool companies to learn what skills and behaviors they want in new people. It gets feedback and follows up on graduates—and has mentors from industry for its students.

It's all about human transformation. Focus: HOPE is about transforming lives. Engineers are taught not only technical skills but work ethic, values, and leadership skills. They are not just trained—they are fundamentally transformed by the Focus: HOPE experience.

Focus: HOPE is an incredible organization. It develops leaders at all levels, and it incorporates Virtuous Teaching Cycles everywhere.

All of the more than fifty thousand volunteers a year, universities, private foundations, governments, local agencies, national agencies, and corporations who partner with Focus: HOPE come away having learned something. The most valuable learnings are about getting people aligned, energized, and working productively.

The good news is that Focus: HOPE proves that it works. The bad news is there's only one Focus: HOPE.

Many people have seen it and talked about replicating it, but none have yet captured its breadth and essence in any meaningful way.

We had MBA teams take a summer and study ways of trying to replicate Focus: HOPE in South Africa, funded by Ford. We had another MBA team go to Northern Ireland to see if a Focus: HOPE could provide a partial solution there. We had an MBA team in East Palo Alto working with Hewlett-Packard, Oracle, and Covad executives to build a Focus: HOPE–like organization.

In fact, many elements of Focus: HOPE have been replicated there and elsewhere, but the world needs thousands of Focus: HOPEs.

■ Learning from the Community: Eleanor's Punch in the Nose

Focus: HOPE was built on the philosophy of the Virtuous Teaching Cycle. After the Detroit riots of 1967, Father Cunningham and Eleanor Josaitis moved into inner-city Detroit—right where the riots occurred. They brought their own Teachable Point of View, captured in their mission statement—"intelligent and practical action to overcome racism, poverty and injustice."

One day, Josaitis had her eye-opening conversation with a seventy-two-year-old woman—the woman, clearly distressed, who wanted to join the food program. "It was a lucky thing that the woman got so angry and starting yelling. It got my attention. I realized that there was a huge need that we were ignoring."

That "aha" changed Josaitis's Teachable Point of View because, "We need to take care of the elderly population." And Focus: HOPE has come up with solution after novel solution ever since.

■ Some Final Reflections

We want to end this chapter with some personal reflections on global corporate citizenship and the future. The challenges for all of us, especially those in senior leadership roles in business, have gone up exponentially. The events of 9/11 and the ongoing war on terrorism have created a new world playing field. It is one that, we believe, makes it a business imperative to lead in new ways.

A way must be found to turn the uncertainty and chaos of the world—the multiple ethnic wars, the global terrorism—into a sustainable, just, and growing global economy.

As if the challenges of building teaching organizations within institutions the size of General Electric, 3M, Home Depot, or Yum! Brands weren't enough, the leaders within institutions now need to reach out and engage the larger communities where they operate in Virtuous Teaching Cycles.

These teaching and learning cycles can help restore the ethics and integrity of American business—and show and share those virtues in the larger communities in which companies operate. By demonstrating their integrity while amplifying their Teachable Point of View on business ethics throughout their company and community, business leaders can begin to forge a new and better image—based on a new and better reality.

After the lapses and transgressions of the early 2000s by some in American business, this leadership renewal is an opportunity—no, a mandate—for all in business to show where they stand, provide lessons to constituents inside and out, and to underscore and renew their own integrity.

For American business to demonstrate such a commitment, there is no better time than now.

Exercises in Ethics

Putting it all together:

1. Review your responses at the end of each chapter and refine and update this listing that you initially prepared after Chapter Three, containing the core elements of your Teachable Point of View.

    a. Ideas:

    _____

    _____

    _____

    _____

    _____

    _____

    b. Values:

    _____

    _____

    _____

    _____

    _____

    _____

    c. Energy:

    _____

    _____

    _____

    _____

    _____

    _____

d. Edge:

_____

_____

_____

_____

_____

_____

2. Use these elements as the basics for revising your Teachable Point
   of View on business ethics. (By the way, it takes months or years
   to master the Teachable Point of View concept, so view this as
   a dynamic creation that will continue to evolve with time and circumstances.) Now write your revised Teachable Point of View on
   business ethics.

_____

_____

_____

_____

_____

_____

_____

_____

_____

_____

_____

_____

_____

_____

_____

_____

_____

_____

_____

3. For your Teachable Point of View on business ethics to take hold and proliferate throughout your organization to produce the Virtuous Teaching Cycle we described at the outset of this book, you'll need a plan.

a. How will you get your team engaged as teachers and learners on business ethics?

_____

_____

_____

_____

_____

_____

b. What is your timetable?

_____

_____

_____

_____

_____

c. What is your first-step commitment—the first thing you will do as a leader-teacher to ensure the successful launch of your Virtuous Teaching Cycle?

_____

_____

_____

_____

_____

4. Good luck! And if things start out less than perfect, keep at it . . . they'll get better with practice and as you and your team create reinforcing Teachable Points of View on business ethics. And congratulations for having the courage to begin this important journey!

Acknowledgments

We are grateful to the many executives and our faculty colleagues at the University of Michigan Business School—people who all have many more pressing demands on their time—for their important and timely contributions to this book.

ServiceMaster's pivotal role in bringing former Secretary of State James A. Baker III to Michigan, along with discussants C. K. Prahalad and Bob Knowling, was a critical starting point.

In simultaneously moving forward on the book and planning the Fall 2002 Orientation of the Michigan Business School Class of 2004, we were able to build on our earlier event. We deeply appreciate CEOs Jeffrey Immelt of GE, James Hackett of Steelcase, Joe Liemandt of Trilogy, and Eleanor Josaitis of Focus: HOPE, for taking on the dual role of coming to Ann Arbor to address our students during Orientation and working with us to develop their chapters for the book. We are especially grateful to our colleague Assistant Dean Graham Mercer and his team for working to make the impact of this important Orientation week as impressive as it became. These events were enhanced by the participation and facilitation efforts of our colleagues

Dean Robert Dolan and Professors Anjan Thakor, Robert Quinn, Kim Cameron, Tim Fort, and LaBrent Chrite, who then went the extra mile in quickly finalizing their book chapters thereafter.

Most of all, we thank the students of the Michigan Business School Class of 2004, whose hard work and candor in examining their own career experiences in preparing for Orientation brought important reality and credibility to their emphasis on ethics in business.

In closing, we are grateful to the people whose daily work made this book possible—our editor and production manager, Kathe Sweeney and Jeff Wyneken of Jossey-Bass, our copyeditor, Hilary Powers, and our assistant Marjorie Heinzman for her countless management of wave after wave of the chapters that comprise this book and related details, and most of all our long-time colleague, Nancy Cardwell, whose skills as an editor and counsel to us in terms of the book's content brought a critical view that enhanced the book's perspective mightily.

Our final appreciation, though, is aimed at all those managers and leaders who live the lessons of ethics every day in their business activities. To them, our thanks for being such fine role models for the rest of us. We hope that, in some small way, this book leads to there being more of you.

The Authors

Noel M. Tichy, Ph.D., is professor of organizational behavior and human resource management at the University of Michigan Business School, where he also directs the Global Leadership Program and codirects the Global Business Partnership, linking global companies and research centers in North America, Japan, and Europe. Between 1985 and 1987, Tichy directed management education at General Electric's worldwide leadership development center in Crotonville, New York. Prior to joining the Michigan faculty he served for nine years on the Columbia University Graduate School of Business faculty. Tichy is the author of numerous books and articles, including *The Cycle of Leadership* (2002), *Corporate Global Citizenship: Doing Business in the Public Eye* (with Andrew R. McGill, 1997), *Every Business Is a Growth Business* (with Ram Charan, 1998), and *The Leadership Engine: How Winning Companies Build Leaders at Every Level* (with Eli Cohen), named one of the top ten business books in 1997 by *Business Week*. Tichy is also coauthor of *Control Your Destiny or Someone Else Will: How Jack Welch Is Making General Electric the World's Most Competitive Company* (with Stratford Sherman). He consults widely in both the private and public sectors, with clients that have included Citibank, Exxon, Pepsico, Honeywell, Hitachi, IBM, Nomura Securities, Oracle, and 3M.

Andrew R. McGill, Ph.D., has a boundary-spanning background as an educator, researcher, consultant, writer, journalist and executive-manager, which he brought to the University of Michigan Business School in 1993 as a professor and codirector of the Global Business Partnership. He developed the courses "Developing the Customer-Driven Organization" and "Human Resources as a Competitive Advantage," is a core faculty member of the school's executive Global Leadership Program, and directs the operations and research activities of a unique affiliation among the Michigan Business School and research universities in Europe and Asia. McGill's research interests focus on the cognitive aspects of organizational change and on organizations becoming more customer-driven. He was instrumental in the launch of Nissan's luxury Infiniti Division. He has consulted to Ameritech, Blue Cross and Blue Shield, Ford, General Motors, Harley-Davison, HarperCollins, Mercedes Benz, Mitsubishi, Royal Bank of Canada, Toshiba, and the Saudi Arabian Monetary Authority. He is coauthor with William H. Newman and E. Kirby Warren of the business textbook *The Process of Management: Strategy, Action, Results*, and coeditor with Noel M. Tichy and Lynda St. Clair of *Corporate Global Citizenship: Doing Business in the Public Eye*, published in 1997.

James A. Baker III, J.D., became the sixty-seventh U.S. Secretary of Treasury on February 3, 1985, and oversaw the collapse of the Iron Curtain and Communism as the 61st Secretary of State, 1989–1992. Prior to that he served as President Reagan's White House chief of staff, a position he occupied from January 1981 through January 1985. While at the White House, Baker also was a member of the National Security Council. He graduated from Princeton University in 1952. After two years of active duty as a lieutenant in the U.S. Marine Corps, he entered the University of Texas School of Law at Austin and received his J.D. with honors in 1957. He still practices law at his family-founded law firm in Houston, Baker & Botts.

Kim S. Cameron, Ph.D., is professor of organizational behavior and human resource management at the University of Michigan Business School and professor of higher education in the School of Education. Cameron's previous research has been on organizational downsizing, organizational effectiveness, corporate quality culture, and the development of leadership excellence. His current research focuses on virtues in organizations, such as forgiveness, humility, and compassion, and their relationships to success. Dr. Cameron received B.S. and M.S. degrees from Brigham Young University and M.A. and Ph.D. degrees from Yale University.

E. LaBrent Chrite, Ph.D., is adjunct assistant professor of corporate strategy at the University of Michigan Business School, where he teaches business strategies and practices to enhance South African development. Dr. Chrite is also managing director of the William Davidson Institute, which studies development in emerging parts of the world, and director of the African Business Development Corps. Chrite earned his B.A. at Michigan State University, his M.S. at the University of Missouri-Columbia, and his Ph.D. at the University of Michigan in 1998. His current interests include alliance strategies in South Africa as well as how firms leverage knowledge for competitive advantage in emerging markets.

Robert J. Dolan, Ph.D., was appointed dean of the University of Michigan Business School in July 2001. Prior to becoming dean and professor, Dolan spent two decades as professor of business administration at the Graduate School of Business Administration at Harvard University. He previously taught at the University of

Chicago and has been a visiting professor at IESE in Barcelona, Spain. Dolan's major research interests are product policy and pricing. He lectures and consults on issues of product policy and pricing to a wide variety of clients.

Tim Fort, J.D., Ph.D., is associate professor of business law and business ethics at the University of Michigan Business School, where he focuses on legal and ethical frameworks that foster ethical business behavior. With Professor Cindy Schipani, he has launched a Corporate Governance and Peace Initiative through the William Davidson Institute, and is also codirector of the Corporate Governance and Corporate Social Responsibility Area of the Davidson Institute. He currently is developing a program in conjunction with the World Bank to provide an interactive, Internet-based dialogue and education program concerning the extent to which businesses can contribute to sustainable peace.

James P. Hackett, B.A., has been president and chief executive officer and director of Steelcase Inc. since December 1994. Steelcase is a leading manufacturer of furniture systems, seating, lighting, storage, architectural and technology products. The company and its subsidiaries have dealers in more than eight hundred locations, manufacturing facilities in more than thirty countries, and approximately twenty thousand employees around the world. Fiscal 2001 revenue was approximately $4 billion. Before joining Steelcase in 1981, Hackett held sales and management positions at Procter & Gamble. He graduated from the University of Michigan in 1977 with a bachelor's degree in general studies. He also played on the UM football team.

Jeffrey R. Immelt, M.B.A., was appointed chairman and chief executive officer of General Electric in 2001, after serving as president and chairman-elect since November 2000, when GE's board selected him to succeed Jack Welch. Immelt began his GE career in 1982 in Corporate Marketing and held a series of leadership roles with GE Plastics in sales, marketing, and global product management, also holding management positions in GE Appliances in an interim period. From 1997 to 2000, Immelt became president and CEO of GE Medical Systems. He holds a B.S. degree in applied mathematics from Dartmouth College and an M.B.A. from Harvard University.

Eleanor M. Josaitis, D.H.L., is chief executive officer of Focus: HOPE, which she co-founded with Father William T. Cunningham (1930–1997) in the aftermath of the 1967 Detroit riots. The metropolitan civil and human rights organization works to eliminate racism, poverty, and injustice primarily by providing access to the financial mainstream through its unique training programs. Josaitis has provided leadership and advocacy since 1971 for Focus: HOPE's Food Program for mothers, children, and senior citizens and has been instrumental in the development of Focus: HOPE's training programs—First Step, FAST TRACK, the Machinist Training Institute, the Center for Advanced Technologies, and the Information Technologies Center. Focus: HOPE also runs a community arts program, business conference facility, and center for children.

Robert E. Knowling Jr., M.B.A., is president of the New York Leadership Academy. He previously served as president of Covad Communications and executive vice president—operations and technologies at US West. At US West, his thirty-thousand-member team was responsible for planning, delivering, and maintaining high-quality telecommunications services for more than 25 million customers in fourteen states. Prior to joining US West, Knowling was vice president—network operations for Ameritech. He received his B.A. from Wabash College, where he was a football All-American, and earned his M.B.A. from Northwestern University's Kellogg Graduate School of Business.

Joe Liemandt is chairman, president, and chief executive officer of Trilogy Software, which he founded in 1989 to capitalize on the enormous opportunity of changing the way high-tech products were bought and sold. Over the past decade, Liemandt has guided Trilogy to become one of the largest private companies in enterprise software. Joe's thought leadership and innovation in e-commerce, as well as in corporate culture and recruiting for the new economy, has been highlighted on the covers of the *Wall Street Journal, Forbes,* and *Fortune,* among others. Joe attended Stanford University, where he majored in economics.

C. William Pollard, J.D., is chairman emeritus of Service-Master—a company specializing in management services for the health care and education markets, and home services for the residential market—which he joined in 1977. ServiceMaster serves more than twelve million customers in the United States and forty-four other countries, with annual revenues of $7 billion. He is actively involved in teaching and speaking on subjects relating to management, ethics, and integrating personal faith with work. Pollard is a graduate of Wheaton College and received his J.D. from Northwestern University School of Law. From 1963 to 1972, he practiced law, specializing in corporate finance and tax matters, and from 1972 to 1977 served on the faculty and as a vice president of Wheaton College.

C. K. Prahalad, D.B.A., is professor of business administration at the University of Michigan Business School, where he specializes in corporate strategy and the role and value added of top management in large, diversified, multinational corporations. A globally acknowledged expert, Professor Prahalad has consulted with the top management in many of the world's foremost companies. Prahalad is also an award-winning author, having won the *Harvard Business Review*'s McArthur Prize for the most influential article of the year.

Robert E. Quinn, Ph.D., is professor of organizational behavior and human resource management at the University of Michigan Business School, where his research focuses on organization effectiveness and leadership. Prior to coming to Michigan, Professor Quinn served on the faculty at the State University of New York at Albany. At Michigan, he teaches in the Ph.D. and M.B.A. programs and in several programs at the school's Executive Education Center. Quinn currently serves as consulting editor for the University of Michigan Business School Management Series, of which this book is a part.

Anjan Thakor, Ph.D., is professor of banking and finance at the University of Michigan Business School, where he is also a popular Executive Education instructor. He also serves as the William Davidson Institute's area faculty director for finance. Professor Thakor came to Michigan from Indiana University, where he served from 1983 to 1996, interrupted by a year on the faculty at UCLA in 1987–88. Professor Thakor earned his Ph.D. from Northwestern University in 1979.

Jonathan P. Ward, B.A., is chairman, president, and chief executive officer of ServiceMaster Company, which currently provides outsourcing services to more than 12 million residential and commercial customers, with combined customer-level revenue of approximately $7 billion. ServiceMaster's core service capabilities include lawn care and landscape maintenance, termite and pest control, plumbing, heating, and air conditioning services, cleaning, furniture repair, and home warranty. Previously, Ward was president and chief operating officer of R.R. Donnelley & Sons. Ward is a graduate of the University of New Hampshire.

Index

Also available in the UMBS series:

Becoming a Better Value Creator, by Anjan V. Thakor

Achieving Success Through Social Capital, by Wayne Baker

Improving Customer Satisfaction, Loyalty, and Profit, by Michael D. Johnson and Anders Gustafsson

The Compensation Solution, by John E. Tropman

Strategic Interviewing, by Richaurd Camp, Mary Vielhaber, and Jack L. Simonetti

Creating the Multicultural Organization, by Taylor Cox

Getting Results, by Clinton O. Longenecker and Jack L. Simonetti

A Company of Leaders, by Gretchen M. Spreitzer and Robert E. Quinn

Managing the Unexpected, by Karl Weick and Kathleen Sutcliffe

Using the Law for Competitive Advantage, by George J. Siedel

Creativity at Work, by Jeff DeGraff and Katherine A. Lawrence

Making I/T Work, by Dennis G. Severance and Jacque Passino

Decision Management, by J. Frank Yates

A Manager's Guide to Employment Law, by Dana M. Muir

For additional information on any of these titles or future titles in the series, visit www.umbsbooks.com.